The
Anatomy of
TONE

Applying Voice Science to
CHORAL ENSEMBLE PEDAGOGY

The
Anatomy of
TONE

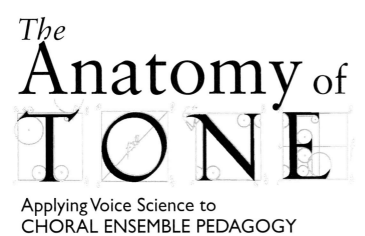

Applying Voice Science to
CHORAL ENSEMBLE PEDAGOGY

JAMES JORDAN
SEAN MCCARTHER
KATHY KESSLER PRICE

with
Corey Everly
Jonathan Palmer Lakeland

GIA Publications, Inc.
Chicago

Other Books by James Jordan
Relating to This Volume

Inside the Choral Rehearsal: Harmonic Rehearsal Teaching and Learning Based on
the Music Learning Theory of Edwin E. Gordon
James Jordan
G-9293

The Complete Choral Warm-Up Sequences
James Jordan
Jesse Borower
with
Brian Sengdala
G-9543

Evoking Sound (Second Edition)
James Jordan
G-7359

The Musician's Breath
James Jordan
Mark Moliterno
Nova Thomas
G-7955

The Choral Warm-Up
James Jordan
G-6397

Structures and Movement of Breathing: A Primer for Choirs
Barbara Conable
G-5265

The Anatomy of Tone:
Applying Voice Science to Choral Ensemble Pedagogy
James Jordan, Sean McCarther, Kathy Kessler Price
with Corey Everly, Jonathan Palmer Lakeland, Amelia Nagoski, Marilyn Shenenberger

Art direction/design: Martha Chlipala

G-9421
ISBN: 978-1-62277-241-4

CONTENTS

PART 3
OVERVIEW OF THE PEDAGOGICAL PLANNING
OF THE CHORAL WARM-UP

PART 4
THE HUMAN CONTENT OF TONE

FOREWORD

This may well be the first book on choral singing with a primary emphasis on voice science: anatomy/physiology and acoustics. The significance of this emphasis begs some scrutiny: Why? And why now? I think the "why" has a few core points. Importantly, as a choral conductor, you may very well be the primary voice expert for most of your singers throughout your career. If you conduct church/synagogue choirs, community choirs, or high school and most college choirs, the majority of your singers look to you for voice instruction. Few choral singers have or will study voice privately; therefore, you become the source of their knowledge for healthy and beautiful singing.

With that responsibility in mind, it makes sense intellectually and ethically that you know as much as possible how to guide your singers' vocal production. Instrumentalists know how their instruments are built. A clarinetist understands reeds and the mechanism of the instrument itself. The violinist can re-string a bow or replace broken strings. Many singers are not aware of how the vocal mechanism is built or works, nor do they adequately understand how it connects to the respiratory system. As a conductor, your instrument is a group of human beings who possess internal, vulnerable instruments. It is your ethical responsibility not to ask for singing that may be harmful to them. Moreover, it makes sense that if your singers are singing in a healthy way with resonant voices, they will produce more pliable, beautiful sounds for you to engage and direct.

Understanding acoustics helps conductors understand the demands that are placed on their singers. When entering a new space, conductors can "pave the way" for singers, understanding how they will need to adjust vocally, arranging the choral spacing to accommodate the acoustical/vocal demands, and making suggestions to help the choristers sing their best. Acoustics matter. This book will help you make a few critical assessments that may invite easier music making in the many venues you and your choirs encounter.

Perhaps the points above comprise the "why," but what about the "why now?" Advances in technology in the last thirty or so years (I know—already quite some time, but still a drop in the musical bucket) have enabled voice scientists and voice teachers to gain intimate knowledge about how the voice works and how it resounds within a space beyond itself. Though knowledge of vocal anatomy/physiology and acoustical theories have existed for centuries, technology now enables singers to see their voices in action, to measure sound pressure levels in performance/rehearsal spaces, and to understand resonance frequencies within the human instrument in ways we never have before. Take advantage of this information! Put it into action to create choirs whose singers do not have to pay the price of over-singing. Enable singers to sing throughout their lifespans with joy and freedom, thereby producing the most exquisite music of which they—and you—are capable.

I am honored to participate as a contributor to this book. I am appreciative of the generosity of spirit that Dr. James Jordan possesses as he invites so many to be a part of a vision of singing that allows choristers to sing in ways that are most comfortable, yet are still musically rich. It is an exciting time to work with choirs of all shapes and sizes, and I applaud you, the reader, for seeking out new information and new challenges. Do not fear voice science—it is here to stay, and it is here to assist you and your singers. Artistry is always the goal. Let's use all the tools we possess to achieve it.

—Kathy Kessler Price, Ph.D.
Westminster Choir College of Rider University

INTRODUCTION

As conductors, we live in the world of choral sound. Few of us realized, however, when we began our journey in choral music that the anatomy of choral tone is both complex and at times elusive. One can choose in one's career to cage it, control it and refine it, or perhaps try to understand how to make it truly reflective of the human condition. The content of choral tone can be as limited or as expansive as the conductor who chooses to guide, cause it, or control it.

Many years ago, Howard Swan, the great choral sage, spoke of the six schools of choral tone in America. His chapter in *Choral Conducting Symposium* was and still is for many of us the categorization and organization of choral sound by both sound and pedagogy. In his chapter, Dr. Swan archived the "schools" of choral tone generated by F. Melius Christiansen, Fred Waring, Robert Shaw, and John Finley Williamson. Much of my professional life has been spent under the long shadow cast by John Finley Williamson. Teaching in a place that was incubated by Williamson, and later re-cast by Frauke Haasemann, the sound of the choirs I conduct has much to do with the past as well as the expressive future of our art. And perhaps there is no other place on the planet where people ponder daily choral sound as it relates to choral performance.

My study in choral pedagogy began with Frauke Haasemann. For whatever reason, Frauke chose me to write the landmark book, *Group Vocal Technique*. In essence, I wrote the book, and then she read it and corrected my errors in pedagogy! I perhaps had the best independent study of any conductor in the twentieth century! As a faithful student, I have tried to carry her teaching forward with my own newfound biases and pedagogies. However, it must be remembered that Frauke and her pedagogy was born in an age before voice science. Hers was a world of trying to bring good singing pedagogy into the choral rehearsal in a non-intimidating way. Further, the pedagogy I had the privilege to document was custom-made for "American amateur singers" (as Frauke like to called them). But as voice science has made its way into voice studio pedagogy, it is my feeling now that we must learn from our colleagues in voice science and move choral pedagogy to higher ground.

This book attempts to give readers an insight into the many components of choral tone through the lens of voice science and then make applications to pedagogy and conducting. The authors also attempt to re-cast the mold on matters such as vowels, breath understandings, resonance, choral standing arrangements. And we also try to tie all of that information into the human content of well-produced vocal sounds. While many may view choral tone as a matter of technique with a debate about pedagogy, my viewpoint may be a bit different. I work daily in a place where choral music and choral sound are at the heart of everything we do. Working with the largest voice faculty in the world creates the potential for a choral ensemble with enormous potential because of the technique and artistry that is taught to our students in the studio. But this place is also an alchemy of tone and spirit unlike any other place in the world. Choral tone, inadvertently, is our patient. Daily rehearsals explore the intersection of tone and human meaning in that tone. From my perspective, it is easy to discuss the vocal/scientific technique and pedagogy that comprises the production of choral sound. It is a bit more challenging, and perhaps a bit more controversial, to open the door of what human factors contribute to choral tone.

When I began my tenure at Westminster as conductor of the Westminster Chapel Choir, I was greeted after one of our tour concerts the second year by an alumnus who had sung in the Westminster Choir under John Finley Williamson. She began the conversation by saying, "Congratulations, you now conduct one of the finest freshman choirs in the world." I felt proud for a few seconds and then I replied, "What do you think will be expected of me here?" She shot back, almost instinctively, "That the sound of the ensembles you conduct be honest."

I have spent my career since that day trying to understand what an "honest" sound is. In many ways, the pursuing of honesty in sound has been my North Star. The vehicle for transport is the sonic character of choral tone. But that sonic character can only be deepened to reflect the human experience and the humans who produce it through alive awareness of both science and spirit that contribute somewhat equal parts to the miracle.

In this book, we organize the pedagogical options in creating a choral sound. Matters of balancing resonance through both production and vowel are necessary understandings. But this book also confronts the human content of tone for each of you to ponder. For me, it is an understanding and awareness of the human expressive element that opens a brilliant world of color and expression. While solo singers certainly understand this aspect of their own sound, it is a bit more difficult to parse when communities of people sing together. The complexity of the content is multiplied by the number of singers involved in the equation and the person in the front of the room. The anatomy, acoustics, and pedagogy of choral tone are easier (and perhaps more simply objective) to deal with because those factors are directly related to clear acoustic science and vocal pedagogy via vocal science. But the human content of tone is a bit more elusive and a bit more challenging.

This book is not proposing a specific path to achieving a certain "sound" in choral tone, although this writer clearly identifies his own biases in the text. Rather, this book is intended to offer conductors a recipe with many ingredients that hopefully will always serve the music and the composer with truth and honesty. Choral sound to the choral conductor should be like the palate of color available to a painter. As choral conductors, we should have access to colors from Monet to Braque, from Rothko to Picasso, and all the variations in between. The hope in writing this book was, in some small way, to lay at your feet a sound world that will allow you to paint more beautiful sound pictures in your ensemble that are equal components of sound and human being. Ultimately, the sound of our choirs and our music should, as the late conductor James DePriest often said, "present a mirror of our better selves."[1]

—James Jordan
Yardley, Pennsylvania

---

1   In James DePriest's obituary, *The New York Times*, February 9, 2013.

PART I
THE SCIENCE OF TONE

CHAPTER 1

THE ANATOMY OF BREATHING

Sean McCarther

I t is safe to say that breathing is important for singing. In fact, many argue that perhaps breathing is the most important component of vocal technique. As my former teacher was fond of saying, "No air, no sound." A properly coordinated breathing technique allows singers to have a flexible vocal production that is equally suitable to the solo stage and the choral ensemble.

Teaching breathing principles or any aspect of vocal technique in the choral environment is a tricky business. At the collegiate or professional level, the task is much easier and often unnecessary. An understanding of basic vocal technique will help these conductors make informed choices and communicate them more clearly to the choir, but they can often assume that either their singers already have a good understanding of their technique or they are working with a private teacher to establish one. Conductors of high school, church, amateur, and civic choruses face a more difficult situation. Often, they are the only person available to guide their singers toward healthy and efficient vocal production. In such cases, it is important that conductors not only have an understanding of how the breathing system works, but also have several ways to help their choirs, *en masse,* coordinate their breaths.

This chapter is a crash course in how the breathing mechanism works and how conductors can explain the basics of good breathing to a group of people with limited risk of misunderstanding and misinterpretation. At the end, I will cover several of the most common myths, misunderstandings, and misinterpretations I have encountered.

THE LUNGS AND LOWER AIRWAY

The lungs are made of a porous, spongy material that is somewhat elastic in nature (its elasticity is an important part of exhalation, but more on that later). The lungs attach to the ribs via two thin pieces of membrane that cause the lungs to stick to the ribs. Because of this connection, any change in the volume of the ribcage causes a similar change in the volume of the lungs. As the lungs get bigger, air rushes in; as the lungs get smaller, air is forced out (*see Figure 1.1*).[2]

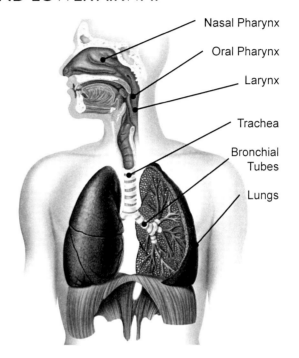

Figure 1.1. Pathway of the air.

Expelled air from the lungs passes through the trachea, past the vocal folds, into the back of the throat, and out the mouth or nose. The trachea is a tube made of flexible cartilaginous rings. The bottom of the trachea splits into two branches, one for the left lung and one for the right lung. If inverted, the trachea forms the trunk of a tree with two main branches: the left lung and the right lung.

The larynx sits at the top of the trachea. Its primary, biological function is to act as a valve to keep food and liquids from falling into the lungs. It is the body's last line of defense against aspiration. Readers probably will have experienced this if they ever swallowed something "down the wrong pipe."

---

2   The physical principle behind inhalation is called *Boyle's Law*. For more information on how this principle affects breathing, consult one of the sources in the reference list at the back of this book. Sources by Richard Miller, Scott McCoy, and Clifton Ware may be particularly useful.

MUSCLES AND BONES

The lungs are housed inside the ribcage, which protects the lungs and other vital organs of the chest. The ribcage is formed of twelve pairs of ribs, all of which originate at the vertebrae of the thoracic (middle and upper) spine (*see Figure 1.2*).

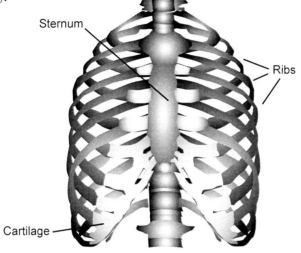

Sternum

Ribs

Cartilage

Figure 1.2. Ribcage.

The top seven pairs of ribs wrap around and connect directly into the sternum, a flat bone in the front of the chest (commonly called the *breastbone*). These seven ribs have very little flexibility and move very little in the breathing process. Ribs 8, 9, and 10 also attach to the sternum but in a more indirect manner. This allows them a fair amount of flexibility. Ribs 11 and 12 do not connect to the sternum. Since the front portion of these ribs "floats" unattached, they are often called the *floating ribs*. They have a substantial amount of flexibility.

Because the lungs attach directly to the ribcage, movement of the ribcage directly influences the volume of the lungs. If the ribcage expands, the volume of the lungs increases and air is inhaled. If the ribcage collapses, the volume of the lungs decreases and air is exhaled. Since neither the lungs nor the ribcage are muscles, they are unable to move on their own. Instead, they must rely on some of the muscles of the chest and thorax to produce movement.

The muscles responsible for moving the lungs can be divided into two groups:

1. Muscles of inhalation
2. Muscles of exhalation

MUSCLES OF INHALATION

The chief muscle of inhalation is the diaphragm (*see Figure 1.3*). Responsible for 60–80 percent of inhalation, the diaphragm receives more attention than any other breathing muscle. It is a dome-shaped muscle that attaches to the base of the sternum, the lower ribs, and the lower spine. When the diaphragm contracts, it flattens several inches. Because the top of the diaphragm attaches to the bottom of the lungs, this contraction pulls the lungs downward, increasing their volume and drawing in air, just as pulling the plunger of a syringe draws in medicine.

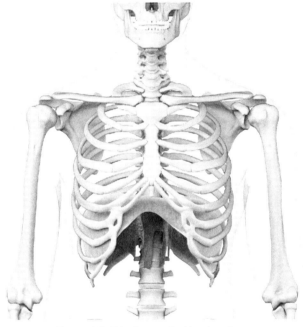

Figure 1.3. Diaphragm inside the ribcage.

Contraction of the diaphragm presses out slightly on the ribcage and presses downward on the organs of the lower abdomen. These organs, called the *abdominal viscera,* are pushed downward and outward, causing the lower abdominal expansion often associated with correct breathing for singing.

The second muscle group of inhalation is the *external intercostals,* which run between each pair of ribs (*see Figure 1.4*). When they contract, they pull the ribcage up and out, expanding the lungs to the sides and causing inhalation. Singers most often feel this expansion as a widening around the lower portion of the ribcage, particularly on the sides.

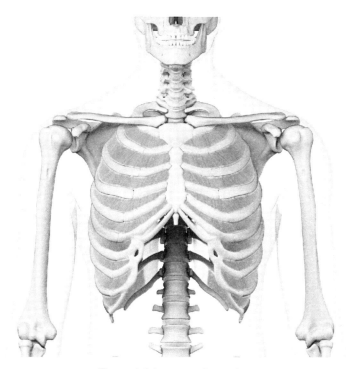

Figure 1.4. Intercostal muscles.
Fibers of the external intercostals run diagonally down and toward midline. Fibers of the internal intercostals run diagonally in a direction opposite of the external intercostal muscles.

MUSCLES OF EXHALATION

The muscles of exhalation include the internal intercostal muscles and the abdominal muscles. The internal intercostal muscles work opposite to the external intercostal muscles. They also run in between the ribs, but when they contract, they pull the ribcage down and in, causing exhalation. Typically, singers only use the internal intercostals at the ends of very long or extremely loud phrases. The powerful contraction of these muscles can easily overblow the vocal mechanism and result in a strident, pressed, or pushed sound.

A more appropriate way to manage exhalation is to use the muscles of the abdominal wall. The *rectus abdominis* (the "six-pack" muscle) connects the sternum to the pelvis (*see Figure 1.5*). When contracted, the rectus abdominis flexes the ribcage downward toward the pelvis (as in a sit-up). While this action is important to stabilize the body during large motions (such as moving a piano), it can collapse the ribcage and limit a singer's ability to take a deep breath. For the singing process, this muscle is generally passive.

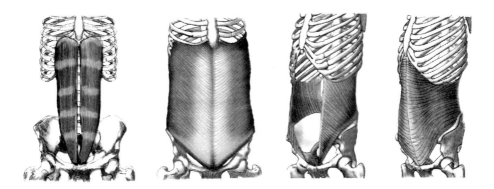

Figure 1.5. (from Left to Right): Rectus Abdominis, External Oblique Abdominis, Internal Oblique Abdominis, Transversus Abdominis.

The internal and external oblique abdominis run diagonally on the sides of the abdomen, connecting the ribcage and the pelvis. When these two muscles contract, they stabilize the pelvis and spine, and also compress the *abdominal viscera* (organs of the lower abdomen). The innermost abdominal muscle is the *transversus abdominis,* which wraps around the body much like a corset. When this muscle contracts, it stabilizes the pelvis, elongates the torso, and compresses the abdomen. At the base of the abdomen are the muscles of the pelvic floor (*see Figure 1.6*). These muscles act like a hammock for the abdominal viscera. They help stabilize the pelvis, and they help the transversus abdominis to compress the abdominal viscera.

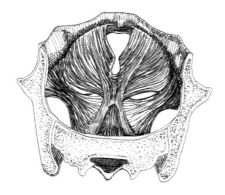

Figure 1.6. Muscles of the pelvic floor.

For breathing, the abdominal muscles work as a team to control exhalation. When the abdominal muscles contract, they press inward and upward on the abdominal viscera, which in turn presses inward and upward on the diaphragm. This reduces the volume of the ribcage and lungs, which causes exhalation. The inward and upward pressure of the muscles of exhalation counters the downward and outward pressure of the muscles of inhalation. This "antagonism" between the muscles of inhalation and the muscles of exhalation gives singers the ability to control the precise amount of air pressure and airflow that reaches the vocal folds. It is a hallmark of the *appoggio* technique (which will be covered later).

THE BREATHING PROCESS

Typically, the breathing process occurs unconsciously and requires very little muscular control or activity. *Passive breathing* (as this is called) occurs in three stages. The process begins with inhalation. During this phase, the diaphragm contracts slightly (approximately 1.5 cm), expanding the lungs. The diaphragm mildly pushes the abdominal viscera out of the way, which results in a slight expansion in the upper stomach area. Normally, the external intercostals remain relatively inactive during passive breathing, but they might become more involved as exertion increases or when more air is needed (e.g., when yawning and sighing). Sometimes, the muscles of the upper chest assist with passive breathing by raising the collarbones and sternum. While this is not necessarily a problem for passive breathing, it is extraordinarily inefficient and not of particular use in the singing process.

The second phase of passive breathing is exhalation. During passive exhalation, the diaphragm relaxes and the lungs, because of their elastic nature, shrink back to their at-rest shape (recall that the lungs are made of a somewhat elastic tissue). As the lungs shrink, air is expelled. The abdominal viscera and the ribcage also return to their at-rest positions. Little, if any, muscular involvement is required in passive exhalation.

The final phase of passive respiration is a brief recovery. If we were to quietly observe our breath, we would notice a slight pause after each exhalation. This pause allows the muscles of respiration a moment of rest.

Breathing for singing involves much more conscious control and occurs in four phases. Like passive breathing, the first phase is inhalation. When one breathes to sing, the diaphragm contracts more deeply than it does in passive breathing, as much as three inches. Additionally, the external intercostal muscles contract to lift and expand the ribcage. The combination of these muscles' actions expands the chest and lungs in all directions (the diaphragm down and the ribcage in the front, to the sides, and a little in the back). Singers sometimes refer to this as a *360° breath,* and it is associated with good singing technique.

The second phase of breathing for an active breath cycle is suspension. The larynx, from a biological viewpoint, serves two purposes: (1) to keep food and liquid out of the lungs and (2) to pressurize the thorax. During intense physical activity (such as heavy lifting), the body will attempt to exhale against the tightly closed vocal folds, pressurizing and stabilizing the torso. (Gym rats who grunt while lifting are using this maneuver.) While this is a necessary response for intense physical activity, it does not allow for a freely produced sound. The suspension phase seeks to counteract the larynx's natural desire to control air pressure within the lungs. During the suspension phase, the glottis (space between the vocal folds) remains open and free while the muscles of inhalation maintain the ribcage's expanded position. Air is neither inhaled nor exhaled. This opens the vocal tract and prepares the singer for the next phase.

The third phase of active breathing is exhalation. During this phase, the muscles of exhalation contract, compressing the abdominal viscera. The viscera are pressed upward against the bottom of the diaphragm which, in turn, presses upward on the lungs, decreasing their volume and expelling air. Singers work to maintain rib expansion for the duration of the sung phrase. The external intercostals, in particular, resist the temptation to relax. In doing so, they keep the ribcage open instead of succumbing to its natural desire to return to a normal, unexpanded state. The temptation to collapse the ribcage is greatest among inexperienced singers who rely on the weight of the ribcage to expel air. This type of exhalation allows very little control over air pressure and causes the ribcage and sternum to come out of alignment. With proper training, singers learn to balance the muscles of inhalation and exhalation to control air pressure and flow to the vocal folds.

The final phase of active breathing is one of brief recovery. Though some repertoire does not allow a singer a chance to rest between phrases, it is ideal to find moments when the breathing system can pause and reset itself. This does not mean that singers should allow the sternum and chest to fall. Instead, singers should maintain their noble posture throughout the singing process.

METHODS OF BREATHING

Since every physical body is different, each singer will organize the muscles and organs of respiration slightly differently. Though the exact configuration will vary, all singers work to find balance in their breathing that allows maximum control over breath pressure and breath flow. Following are the four most common ways people generally organize the breathing system:

1.   Clavicular breathing
2.   Costal breathing
3.   Abdominal breathing
4.   Diaphragmatic/Costal breathing

CLAVICULAR BREATHING

Clavicular breathing relies on the muscles of the chest, shoulders, upper back, and neck to raise the upper ribcage and chest for each inhalation. The upper chest and lungs expand, resulting in inhalation. Once these muscles relax, the ribcage collapses to its pre-breath position, decreasing the dimensions of the upper chest and expelling air from the lungs. This method of breathing is extremely prevalent in untrained or beginning singers.

While clavicular breathing does allow the exchange of carbon dioxide for oxygen, keeping one alive, it offers little added benefit for singers. The amount of muscle required to raise the ribcage is extraordinarily fatiguing. Additionally, the speed with which the chest collapses after inhalation expels the air rapidly and with little control. This method will generally limit the descent of the diaphragm and not allow a singer to take a full, complete breath. Responding to this lack of air, the vocal folds will either fail to close completely (producing a breathy sound) or succumb to their biologically programmed response to act like a valve, closing too tightly and producing a tight or pinched sound.

COSTAL BREATHING

Costal breathing places emphasis on ribcage expansion. The external intercostal muscles expand the ribcage in all directions, particularly the sides and back. When properly executed, the diaphragm descends completely and the singer is able to control breath flow and pressure during exhalation.

Costal breathing is also a method of breathing used by many fitness programs (e.g., Pilates) because it allows the transverse abdominis to remain contracted during the entire breathing cycle and provides more stability to the pelvis and spine. Though not in and of itself a problem, it can encourage some people to limit the descent of the diaphragm, particularly those with a strong background in fitness. As with clavicular breathing, the limited diaphragmatic descent does not allow for a full and complete breath. Additionally, the abdominal muscles may over-contract, which reduces a singer's ability to control breath pressure and flow during exhalation. Teachers who advocate this method of breathing should be on the lookout for tight abdominal muscles or excessive expansion of the ribcage, which causes tension. Additionally, they should listen to make sure the sound remains supple, flexible, and vibrant. Over-contraction of the abdominal wall disrupts the consistency of the airstream and can lead to pressed, pushed, straight, or wobbly tone production.

ABDOMINAL BREATHING

Abdominal breathing is sometimes referred to as "belly breathing." Singers emphasize the release of the lower abdominals, which allows the diaphragm to descend fully. In many cases, this causes the lower stomach (or belly) to protrude during each inhalation. This method of breathing can be very helpful for singers whose "go to" breathing habit is clavicular breathing: it is easy to see and feel, and it is a viable alternative to clavicular breathing. It can also be helpful for singers who lack a sense of grounding or depth in their breathing.

Teachers who advocate this method of breathing must be cautious, however. The sole focus on abdominal expansion can neglect the importance of the ribcage in the breathing process and, in extreme cases, can cause the larynx to lock. Encourage singers to maintain proper body alignment since excessive protrusion of the abdomen can cause slouching. Additionally, in certain studios, some singers are taught to forcibly push the stomach out during inhalation and exhalation. This abdominal tension (often labeled "locking") can result in over-pressurization of the vocal mechanism and laryngeal tension. The result is often a pinched, pressed, or forced sound.

DIAPHRAGMATIC/COSTAL BREATHING

Diaphragmatic/Costal breathing allows the full descent of the diaphragm and the expansion of the ribcage. It is sometimes called *combined breathing* or *balanced breathing* because it combines the best qualities of costal and abdominal breathing. The abdominal muscles relax during inhalation and gently engage during exhalation. The external intercostals expand the ribcage for inhalation and then work to keep it expanded during exhalation. By keeping the ribcage open, the external intercostals allow the abdominal muscles to take on the bulk of exhalatory control. In this way, a singer is able to take a full, complete breath and control how that breath is used in the singing process. This is the method of breathing taught in the Italian School of singing and is often referred to as *appoggio.*

APPOGGIO

The term *appoggio* comes from the Italian words *appoggiarsi a* ("to lean upon") and is one of the hallmarks of the Italian School of singing. Richard Miller gives this definition of the term:

> *Appoggio* cannot narrowly be defined as "breath support," as is sometimes thought, because *appoggio* includes resonance factors as well as breath management…. The historic Italian School did not separate the motor and resonance facets of phonation as have some other pedagogies. *Appoggio* is a system for combining and balancing muscles and organs of the trunk and neck, controlling their relationships to the supraglottal resonators, so that no exaggerated function of any one of them upsets the whole.[3]

Two points from this quotation are important. First, *appoggio* is not solely a breathing concept. It refers to the entire vocal mechanism and has implications for posture, breathing, phonation, resonance, and articulation. As I tell my students, "Nothing functions in isolation." Second, the goal from a breathing perspective is to balance the muscles of inhalation and exhalation in such a way that the singer has complete control over how much air reaches the vocal folds, at what speed, and with what amount of pressure.

---

3   Richard Miller, *The Structure of Singing: System and Art in Vocal Technique* (Belmont, CA: Schirmer, 1996), 23.

For *appoggio* breathing, singers must first find a proper alignment of the head, neck, and ribcage. This alignment allows the ribs to expand and the diaphragm to descend properly. Additionally, the elevated ribcage provides a stable foundation for the muscles that connect the chest and the larynx (the infralaryngeal muscles). This helps to position the larynx comfortably low within the neck and provides stability to the entire laryngeal mechanism. Singers maintain this comfortably elevated ribcage position throughout the breathing cycle.

During inhalation, the ribcage expands to the front and sides, and slightly to the back. The diaphragm descends, displacing the abdominal viscera, which causes the stomach to expand. As Miller describes, "The region between the sternum and the umbilicus moves outward on inspiration, but the chief outward movement occurs in the lateral planes."[4]

At the start of exhalation, singers should feel no sense of grabbing or holding in the throat. This inhibits the biologically programmed response of the larynx to act as a valve; the larynx and throat should remain open and free. The chest and sternum should remain comfortably elevated during the entire phrase, and the ribcage should remain relatively expanded. Obviously, the lateral expansion will fall toward the end of each phrase, but the student should work to keep this expanded as long as is comfortable. The overall position of the torso should be the same at the end of each phrase as it was at the beginning: "Posture need not be altered for the renewal of breath."[5]

ADDRESSING BREATHING IN THE CHORAL ENVIRONMENT

I typically address breathing in the following order, making sure students understand my expectations in each before moving on to the next.

1. Alignment
2. Inhalation – how the breath comes into the body
3. Exhalation – how the breath leaves the body to create tone

I have listed a few ideas, images, metaphors, and exercises that can be useful to promote change in each of these areas. Many of the exercises and metaphors described are not new (in fact, several have been around for centuries). However, it is important that conductors and private instructors alike understand the anatomical and physiological principles that underpin each exercise and

---

4   Ibid., 24–25.
5   Ibid., 25.

metaphor. This information ensures that the cues we give our students are targeted rather than the proverbial shot in the dark. Obviously, not all images will work for all groups, but armed with a firm physiological understanding, choir directors should be able to modify and adapt most exercises to suit the needs of their ensembles.

PHYSICAL ALIGNMENT[6]

The first step in establishing a good breathing technique is to ensure that the body is aligned correctly. Without correct alignment, the ribs cannot expand, the diaphragm cannot lower, and singers lose their ability to control the airstream.

Feet:

The feet should be placed underneath the hip joints and may turn out slightly. Most people stand with their feet underneath the outside edge of their hips, not directly under the hip joint. This results in a stance that is a little too wide.

You might also think of the feet as tripods with a point on the heel, a point on the mound of the big toe, and a point on the mound of the little toe. Gently rock in a circular motion until weight rests equally on all three points.

Bend, Bend, Bend:

There should be a slight bend or softening in the ankles, behind the knees, and in the hips. In general, most people are very tight in their hips, and many lock their knees. To help find these easy bends, bend deeply at the knees and notice the creases in the ankles, knees, and hips. Return to standing upright, but try to maintain that sense of softness in those three areas.

Pelvis:

Neutrality of the pelvis is incredibly important for proper alignment of the spine. The two main misalignments of the pelvis are to tip it too far forward (the more common) or to tip it too far back. It is nearly impossible to address this issue in a group since each individual will require a different cue. However, there are a few general comments to make.[7]

---

6   For more detailed information on the anatomy of alignment, consult one of the sources in the Bibliography and Resource List at the back of this book. The two-part article series, Sean McCarther, *Being Careful with Cueing,* is particularly applicable.

7   Often, properly grounding the feet can bring the pelvis into correct alignment. For more information on grounding the feet and legs, I highly recommend the DVD *Voice at the Center* by Ruth Williams Hennessy.

- Think of a gentle wave of energy traveling up the front of the thighs. This energy catches the pelvis and pulls up the front portion. You might also envision a balloon attached to the pubic bone pulling the pelvis up in the front.

- With your hands, brush up the front of your pelvis, over the top of the hips, and gently down the back. This "current of the pelvis" is a physical and mental image that can help the pelvis find neutrality.

I typically advise against the cue, "Tuck your tailbone." Often, singers will over-contract the hamstrings and gluteal muscles, resulting in a lot of tension in the lower back. This tension restricts the ability of the lower ribcage to expand and inhibits the breathing process.

Ribcage and Shoulders:

The ribcage should find a comfortably high position. This so-called "noble posture" allows the ribcage and diaphragm to expand completely during inhalation. Typically, inexperienced singers will stand with the ribcage and sternum (breastbone) collapsed. Be on the lookout for this collapsed posture and be ready to offer alternatives:

- Raise your arms over your head. Feel where your sternum and ribcage are. Allow your arms to pivot in the socket to come back to normal, but leave the ribcage in this comfortably high position.

- Think of the chest as a box. To open and elevate the chest, lift the entire box (not just the front). Otherwise, the box will tilt backward (i.e., raising the sternum and collapsing the back).

- Remember to be as wide across the back as you are across the front. Many people collapse the back to find width in the front.

I typically advise against the cue, "Shoulders back and down." While this can be a useful cue, many students go too far and end up depressing their shoulder blades. Their alignment might appear to be correct from the front, but the muscles of the back will be tight and they will limit the ability of the ribcage to expand during the breathing process.

Head and Neck:

In general, cues regarding the head and neck should encourage a lift of the entire head, not just one portion. Pay particular attention to singers during ascending scales or passages with a higher tessitura. Often, young singers will begin to stick out their chin and tilt their head back in an attempt to sing higher notes. Be ready to offer alternatives:

- Imagine that a horizontal plate extends through the center of your head at the level of your eyes. Imagine that a marble is placed in the center of that plate. Very slowly, imagine that you could move your head to roll the marble in a circle around the plate.

- Use your nose to draw tiny circles in the air. Similarly, imagine that a pencil extends from the top of your head toward the ceiling. Move your head so this imaginary pencil draws circles on the ceiling.

- Have a partner use the backs of his/her fingers to gently brush upward from your cheekbones, across the temples, and up the head. Be sure this does not pull the front of the head forward or up. The entire head should lengthen upward.

INHALATION

As was stated earlier in this chapter, during inhalation, the diaphragm descends and the ribcage expands to the sides and slightly in the back. Below are a few exercises and images to help students understand what it means to take a "low breath."

1. **The "thinker" position** – Have singers sit in a chair with elbows on knees and cheeks resting on hands. Ask the singers to breathe in slowly through their noses. In this position, it is very difficult to raise the shoulders during inhalation. Singers can focus on the expansion of the sides of their bodies and their backs.

2. **Breathing into the hands or thumbs** – Ask singers to place their hands or their thumbs into the space between the hip and lower

ribcage. Singers should then think only of expanding so the hands move out. They do not need to think about pulling air in: as they expand, air will be drawn in passively.

3. **Bouncing epigastrium** – The epigastrium is the "squishy" area directly beneath the sternum. Ask singers to find a comfortably elevated sternum and place a hand on the epigastrium. Then ask them to pant like a dog. The epigastrium should bounce slightly with each breath. This is a great way to teach singers to release the abdominal muscles during the exhalation process, and it prevents abdominal locking.

4. **Mushroom breath** – Imagine that the breath is an upside-down mushroom cloud. There is a thin "stalk" from the neck down toward the abdomen, which then expands down and to the sides.

5. **Ping-pong ball breath** – Imagine there is a ping-pong ball, a plastic Easter egg, or something similar at the base of the spine. During inhalation, singers should breathe as if they could fill the ping-pong ball with air.

6. **Temperature of the air** – Ask singers to take a slow inhalation through the nose but with the mouth open. Ask them to imagine that the air curls across the roof of the mouth before going deep into the body. Draw their attention to the cooling sensation of the air as it is slowly drawn into the body.

WATCH OUT! INHALATION

There are a few myths, misconceptions, or general "faults" that often accompany inhalation. I would like to address the most common.

1. **"Take a deep breath"** – So much of the success of students in my studio hinges upon establishing a mutually understood vocabulary. As I have said to students in the past, "I want to make sure that when I say *dog*, you understand I mean *cat*." Instructions such as "take a deep breath" are perfectly valid as long as students understand what it means in their own body to take a "deep" breath. If there is a misunderstanding as to what this actually means,

students may resort to clavicular (shoulder) breathing, abdominal (belly) breathing, or they may simply take in too much air.

2. **"Breathe low"** – This is similar to the phrase, "Take a deep breath." Before using this phrase, be sure everybody in the choir understands what it means to "breathe low." It might be a good idea to begin every rehearsal with an exercise or image that reminds the choir what inhalation for singing means.

3. **"I need more air to sing longer phrases"** – It is more important for singers to use the air they have well than to take in too much air. Inhaling too much air in an attempt to sing a longer phrase makes all the muscles of breathing tense. The muscles are then unable to respond fluidly to the demands of the musical phrase and often create a pinched or pressed sound that still does not make it through the entire phrase. For students with this issue, I often recommend taking a "sip" of air. Once they take in an appropriate (and smaller) amount of air, they are usually able to easily sing through the phrase, and the sound often improves.

4. **Shoulder breathers** – Clavicular (shoulder) breathing is incredibly prevalent among beginning or amateur singers. It is a typical and appropriate way to breathe during everyday life; however, it is very limiting for singers. This kind of breathing should be rather easy to spot. It is important to give these singers a more efficient model for inhalation. Several of the exercises listed above will be helpful.

5. **Belly breathers** – Abdominal (belly) breathing typically occurs in students who have some training or experience singing. In an attempt to take a "deep" breath, students over- expand the abdomen and belly during inhalation. Though this does allow a full descent of the diaphragm, it can cause excessive tension in the abdomen and often leads to slouching. Additionally, this kind of breathing can destabilize the larynx. For these singers, compliment the work they are doing to take a low breath, but ask that they start to think about expanding the sides and ribcage as well, leading to a more 360-degree breath.

EXHALATION

During exhalation, singers work to keep the ribcage expanding so it does not collapse quickly. This allows the abdominal muscles to remain pliable so they can adjust to the changing air demands of the sung phrase. Below are a few exercises, images, and metaphors that will help singers use their air in the most efficient manner:

1. **Standing in a barrel** – Ask singers to imagine they are standing inside a barrel. When they inhale, they should try to expand and touch all sides of the barrel. As they exhale, they should continue to touch the sides of the barrel.

2. **Wave breath** – Imagine that the breath is like a wave. Just as a wave will form until the moment it crests, so, too, the breath is inhaled until the moment of exhalation. Ask singers to inhale until comfortably full. It is sometimes helpful to have them engage the entire body by rocking gently back and forth. As soon as they are comfortably full, ask them to exhale. Again, it is often helpful to engage the body by having the singers rock forward along with the breath gesture. The physical motion of rocking back and forth should be smooth and fluid. In this exercise, it is important that the singers begin to feel a natural rhythm to the breath. The breath is either coming in or going out. There is no catch before the exhalation.

3. **Hissing** – Hissing is a great way to help singers work on exhalation. Singers need to work on both high-pressure and high-flow airstreams. Hissing can help with this. For high pressure, ask the singers to make a hiss with a high pitch. For high flow, ask the singers to make a hiss with a low pitch.

   CAUTION: Make sure the singers are not gripping in the throat to make either of these hisses. The throat should remain open and free so the muscles of breathing bear the workload. Be sure the airstream remains constant and does not surge, louder one moment and softer the next.

4. **Speed of air** – I often use miles per hour to talk about the speed of my students' air. Higher notes require faster air, but we cannot suddenly slam on the gas. Instead, we need to gradually increase the speed of our air as we ascend in pitch. This keeps singers from "punching" high notes and encourages legato singing and even registration. Students can practice this by simply blowing air, with a pinwheel or other similar "toy."

5. **Vocalization** – Vocalizing singers on lip trills, tongue trills, raspberries, and certain consonants (such as [s], [f], [θ], [z], [v], [ð]) can be very helpful in establishing good breathing technique.

6. **Onsets** – Onsets are a great way to coordinate the breathing process. Begin with five quarter-note pulses on the same pitch, taking a breath between each initiation of sound and the next. Adjust the speed as necessary so the singers have time for a good inhalation. As the singers become more adept, increase the speed of the pulses, eventually moving to nine eighth-note pulses, still keeping a breath between each one. Emphasis should be placed on clarity and vibrancy on tone regardless of the note's duration.

WATCH OUT! EXHALATION

There are a few myths, misconceptions, or general faults that often accompany exhalation. I would like to address a few of those.

1. **More support fixes every problem** – Many singers think that if their voice is not working correctly, they need to "support" the sound more. Generally, this is accompanied with a vague sense to push more. Typically, the answer is not a matter of needing more of anything. Rather, it is about finding a balance that works well for each individual singer. Agility and onset exercises are a great way to help singers find this balance intrinsically. When in doubt, refer the singer to a teacher.

2. **More air fixes every problem** – As with the idea that more support fixes every vocal problem, some people believe that more air is always the key. Again, finding an appropriate balance between

air pressure and airflow is the important step. Exercises that use voiced or unvoiced consonants, nasal consonants, lip trills, tongue trills, and onsets can be helpful in establishing this balance.

3. **Relax everything** – The generic cue to relax is not always helpful. Singing requires a fair amount of work and energy of the body. By establishing an efficient alignment and teaching good breathing habits, we can help singers discover the difference between necessary and unnecessary tension. The exercises above for alignment as well as those found in some of the resources in the Bibliography and Resource List in the back of this book can be helpful.

4. **Singing loud and soft** – The primary, biological function of the larynx is to keep food and liquid out of the lungs. It is, therefore, very good at closing tightly to protect the airway. This is, obviously, bad for singing. We work to inhibit this biologically programmed response so the vocal folds release and vibrate freely. When singers do not provide the vocal folds with an appropriate airstream (too much air or too little), the vocal folds grip, producing a pressed and pinched sound. This means each singer will have a maximum and a minimum dynamic level, above and below which they are incapable of creating a free and, more importantly, healthy sound. Continually asking singers to sing softer may not only produce a less harmonically rich sound but may, in fact, be damaging or at the least fatiguing to the singers. Similarly, singers in large choirs or in choirs accompanied by loud instruments (such as organ) are less likely to self-monitor and may over-sing. Encourage singers only to produce sounds that are comfortably within their voice.

CHAPTER 2
GOOD VIBRATIONS:
VOCAL RESONANCE IN CHORAL SINGING

Kathy Kessler Price

Artistry begins when we can be heard.

—attributed to Oren Brown,
voice pedagogue (1909–2004)

Singers invest their voices, energies, time, and treasure to become the best singers they can be. Those who seek the art of singing as a profession spend countless hours and dollars in lessons, coaching, practice sessions, and rehearsals to explore and imprint the techniques that unlock their expressive capabilities. Singers who are more avocational might also study with private teachers to improve their "solo" voices, but often they do so to simply and unselfishly become better "choral" singers. Certainly, they also expend hours of their lives in "choir practice," where they not only sing and listen but also wait patiently while the other voices rehearse their parts. Whether solo or choral or both, vocal musicians have a passion for their art and craft that is built on the most human of all arts—singing.

With so much time and effort given, it is only fitting that singers are rewarded with the joyful knowledge that their best efforts have been heard in the ways they have prepared for and expect. Singers should be able to count on the fact that their voice teachers, coaches, and conductors are their partners in seeking optimum acoustical approaches to ensure just that. Those approaches include each singer's individual resonant capabilities, fully realized, and the advantageous use of the acoustical venue. Assuming the singers have vocally prepared the performance piece to be as resonant as possible, they should be able to depend on that preparation wherever the performance occurs. Yet, how often have we exquisitely prepared a piece only to have to throw out all nuances when we get to the stage because the acoustical environment is completely different than where we rehearsed? How frustrating it is to resort to singing as loudly as possible or with unrehearsed detachment for each pitch to produce sound that is audible and clean! And how much worse to sing an entire concert that no one adequately hears!

What knowledge can save us from these situations? Are there areas that are often not considered when we study, rehearse, and then move from a period of intense preparation to anticipating a performance? I believe there are. This knowledge has several components—many well known, but sometimes forgotten in the last-minute rush to the finish line of the performance date. Some of this knowledge is scientific and may not be familiar to everyone, but it can be easily disseminated and understood via today's many resources (e.g., the internet, journals, books, etc.). The next few chapters are devoted to the topic of vocal acoustics (both solo and choral) and how singers and conductors can make the most of them.

VOCAL RESONANCE

Clearly there is something quite unusual about the voice of a first-class opera singer. Quite apart from the music, the intrinsic quality of such a voice can have a forceful impact on the listener. Moreover, a well-trained singer produces sounds that can be heard distinctly in a large opera house even over a high level of sound from the orchestra, and can do so week after week, year after year. If a second-rate singer or a completely untrained one tried to be heard over an orchestra, the result would be a scream and the singer's voice would soon fail.

—Johan Sundberg,
The Acoustics of the Singing Voice (1977)

We may or may not possess the voice of a "first-class opera singer" as Sundberg (b. 1936), musicologist and musical acoustician, describes above, but the very resonant nature he describes can be a part of what every singer brings to music making. Resonance is part and parcel of timbre, beauty, power, diction, and even audibility for every voice. To understand how to attain resonance, it is necessary to take a glimpse into how vocal sound begins and how it builds into vibrant tone.

CREATING VOCAL SOUND

For a sound to start, the brain, breath, and muscles get to work to create vibration. The brain sends a signal to the intrinsic (inner) muscles of the larynx, and they respond by closing the vocal folds (cords) after inhaling. In other words, the first thing that happens after taking in a breath is the vocal folds meet at the mid-line of the glottis (space between folds) and gently touch down the length of each fold. A simpler description would be of two narrow, three-dimensional, horizontal bands meeting each other down their full length. Virtually simultaneously, breath pressure begins to build below the closed folds. When that pressure reaches a certain threshold (needed to produce the pitch and dynamic the singer intends), the folds part in an undulating fashion, bottom to top, known as the *mucosal wave*. The air pressure beneath the folds then becomes less as it moves past and between the open folds until it needs to be renewed to keep up this process. Therefore, the folds close again via muscles, inertia, and the Bernoulli Effect to build air pressure, and the cycle repeats. All these activities occur within fractions of a second. For instance, at the pitch A440 (what we commonly tune to) the folds are oscillating 440 times per second! As these vibrating folds and air pressure combine, pitch is created—whatever the ear and brain have coordinated beforehand—as the folds are contracted or stretched for lower or higher pitches.

Without making this too much of an anatomy lesson, it is also good to know that two sets of muscles inside the larynx balance each other continually to govern pitch. They are the *thyroarytenoid muscles (TA)*, which constitute the main muscle body of the folds themselves and are responsible for lower pitches, and the *cricothyroid muscles (CT)*, which contract to tilt the thyroid cartilage (felt as one's Adam's Apple) down and slightly forward toward the base of the larynx (cricoid cartilage), thereby stretching the folds for higher pitches. These two muscle groups are in constant cooperation with each other to finely tune the folds to produce the frequency and degree of loudness the singer is requesting. Indeed, the TA muscles also increase the bulk of the folds for louder sounds, and the CT muscles help thin for softer sounds. For lower pitches, the TA muscles are dominant; for higher pitches, the CT muscles may become dominant, especially for women. Indeed, when sopranos and altos (choral designations) sing in "head" voice, they are CT dominant, and when they are in "chest" voice, they are TA dominant. Tenors, baritones, and basses sing in TA dominance throughout their ranges, unless they move into falsetto, which is CT dominant.

The often difficult "mix" for men (some call this *head voice*) is tricky because of the need to maintain TA dominance when the voice would innately prefer to switch to CT dominance. This adjustment is similar to "belt" for female singers in contemporary commercial music (CCM). Western Classical music culture has decided, roughly over the last century and a half, that men maintaining TA dominance in their higher pitches is exciting and visceral—and preferred. So men (singing as tenors, baritones, and basses) must do it or be pioneers and start a new trend. However, for absolutely everyone, both muscle groups are at work all the time to create pitch and the nuance of dynamics (soft to loud) without our direct awareness. How amazing the vocal instrument is!

Pitch, or frequency, for singing is never a simple, single sound wave. It is a complex sound, not a sine wave alone, made up of a fundamental frequency (abbreviated as *Fo*—that which we hear as the actual pitch) and its accompanying harmonics or overtones. The vocal folds produce many harmonics as well as the fundamental pitch. (To be precise, the fundamental frequency is considered the first harmonic. The second harmonic, however, is considered the first overtone.) All these frequencies—fundamental and harmonics (overtones)—emit from the vocal folds themselves. There is not a beauty of tone yet, but the actual pitch with harmonics is present thanks to these vibrating wonders. The vocal folds, then, are considered the "source" of the sung tone.

To become enriched, resonant, and colorful, these frequencies have to travel through a filter known as the *vocal tract* (the spaces above the folds) until the singing tone exits the lips. Indeed, the unique shape of each person's vocal tract creates that individual's personal vocal color. That color or timbre is what identifies *your* voice—why friends recognize you on the phone, or why you can identify a famous singer's voice on a recording. Resonance is primarily enhanced, however, by the way each person *shapes* his/her vocal tract (position of the larynx, pharynx, and mouth/tongue/palate/lips) to form words and tone. The vocal tract is primarily the spaces in the pharynx (throat) and mouth with all the accompanying inhabitants, especially the tongue, the lips, and the degree of jaw release controlling the shaping of those spaces to various degrees. As the frequencies travel through this tract, some sound waves are selected for success and some fail to make the entire trip. If the tract is well shaped for the desired vowel and vocal color, and the vocal folds are doing their job of clean closure in vibratory mode, then sound waves will become reverberant. If not, those waves not matching the vocal tract shape will either die off or be heard as noise in the vocal sound.

The most influential shaper in the tract is the tongue; hence, that is why voice teachers continually admonish singers to find tongue release, ensure the tip is gently touching, when possible, the front, lower teeth, and on and on. I call the tongue *"The Beast"* with good reason! It is difficult to know what it is doing unless we feel the tip touching the gum line or teeth and/or we look in a mirror as we sing. Once singers discover what it feels like to have a freely released tongue, they can replicate it. However, singers must constantly be aware of its role to keep it in good order. The tongue seems to have a mind of its own.

As we begin exploring resonance through the vocal tract, it is important to understand a bit more about perceived resonance. We singers are often led astray, as we hear ourselves differently than does the rest of the world. Almost everyone has experienced hearing one's own voice on a recording and being astonished that we sound differently than we thought. We share that first disbelief when we exclaim, "That's not how I sound, is it?" Our primary sense of resonance comes from the connection between the vibrating instrument (the vocal folds in the somewhat mobile larynx) and the rest of our body. We feel that sensation as forced resonance (bone and tissue vibrating), and it is audible to us. Everyone else hears us through free resonance, or sound waves traveling through air in our vocal tracts and then out into the surrounding space. Of course, our ears as singers inform our perception of our voices as well, particularly in areas of intonation, loudness, diction, and timbre. This mode of assessment is called the *auditory feedback loop,* and it is critical to singing success. However, for reliable vocal production, singers must depend on the *sensations* of sound for feedback while understanding that the timbre others hear is somewhat different from their own perceptions.

FORMANTS

When I was a child, Mama had the best voice of all the members of the church. She had loved to sing. Her words had soared like an angel's over the swells of the organ.

—Siri Mitchell,
She Walks in Beauty

In the quote above, "Mama" definitely had a good grasp of resonance and understood instinctively something voice science calls *formants*. A formant for singing is an area in the vocal tract that holds potential for resonance. The shapes of the tract create these areas of resonant energy that love certain frequencies, but not others. Formants "like" the range of frequencies that correspond to their shapes. When the frequencies (sound waves) that a particular formant area accepts pass through it, those frequencies meet a welcome environment and travel all the way to eventually exit as singing sound. When frequencies pass through formant areas that are not compatible, they are usually dampened. Though there are many potential formants, singers have only five useful formant areas (abbreviated as F1, F2, F3, F4, and F5) in the vocal tract. If we travel up the vocal tract, beginning with the larynx, we can visualize where each of these formants resides.

The areas of the epilarynx (between the vocal folds and the epiglottis) support higher overtones, which voice science labels formants 4 and 5 (F4, F5). The upper pharynx and back of the oral cavity (mouth) support the first formant (F1), which is the home of warmer, rounder, more vertical sound, especially if the soft palate is raised. The mid to front of the mouth supports formant 2 (F2), which is the zone of more brilliant, brighter sound. From the tip of the tongue forward to the teeth is the third formant (F3). Since this is such a small space, we generally say that F3 contributes to overall resonance, much like F4 and F5. Indeed, the combination of these three formants (F3, F4, and F5) are often referred to as the *Singer's Formant* (more about that in a coming paragraph).

Formants 1 and 2 are responsible for the color, distinction, and intelligibility of vowels. All vowels consist of a mixture of these two formant frequencies. A vowel high in F1 value will have a warmer, darker, rounder timbre—such as /ɑ/ or /ʌ/. A vowel rich in F2 value will have a brighter, more forward, edgier timbre—such as /i/ or /e/. Practically speaking, the longer the vocal tract (consisting of a lowered larynx, a tall pharynx, a lowered jaw, and slightly protruding lips) the more F1 value there will be. A slightly higher larynx, a smaller mouth opening, and perhaps slightly spread lips will raise F2 with its bright, ringing, and sometimes brassier tone.

Formants 3–5 enhance resonance generally (rather than defining vowels) and form what is known as the *Singer's Formant*. Many singers who otherwise may not be aware of formants have, nonetheless, heard of this impressive term. The Singer's Formant is what gives a professional singer's voice its characteristic ring and power. It is often described as the resonance that enables a singer to be heard over an orchestra. Some choral conductors are concerned that the Singer's Formant, given free reign, would create a chorus of solo singers, not the cohesive sound they might prefer. However, recent research (examined in Chapter 6: Good Vibrations: Choral Spacing) reveals that this fear may be a needless worry.

Singers continually mold these various formant areas (potential resonance) by the way they position the tongue, lips, jaw, etc., yet they are generally unaware of their acoustical properties. It is an intuitive process. We singers respond to auditory and sensory feedback and, of course, sing through muscle memory as we have practiced. Because tenors, baritones, and basses, and to a lesser degree lower alto voices, have many more audible harmonics than higher treble voices (because they start out lower), they can use more of the sensory perception of the Singer's Formant. Sopranos' fundamental frequencies begin much higher, thereby shifting their audible overtones beyond the useful range of the Singer's Formant. Sopranos of all sorts must try a different strategy. This strategy is called *formant tuning* or *vowel modification*. All singers can and should avail themselves of this strategy, but higher treble voices must do so to avoid shrill, piercing sounds that also feel uncomfortable to the singers.

Formant tuning implies that singers have changed the frequency range of a formant area to bring it closer to a nearby harmonic. Singers accomplish this task by changing the vocal tract shape. When the formant area is in close proximity to the harmonic's frequency, the harmonic is boosted and a more resonant sound is produced.

With sopranos, formant tuning often involves tuning more to the fundamental frequency (Fo) since it is already a high pitch, rather than even higher harmonics. Choral conductors often support this technique, as they want the audience to hear the melodic pitch clearly. To achieve this tuning, sopranos must release their jaws, create more space, and open the vowels (vowel modification) as their singing moves to G5 and above. Vowel modification is the name of the game, whether singers are consciously aware of the progression of vowel adjustments or they are merely releasing the jaw more and more. The effect is the same. This technique enables the soprano voice to have greater resonant power, even without the aid of the Singer's Formant. However, when the mouth is more open and the jaw fully released in a soprano's head voice, there is not as much internal feedback provided to the singer. The sensory perception of bone conduction and vibrations within the pharynx and mouth are not as great as for lower voices. Therefore, sopranos, in particular, must have space outside themselves in which to hear their voices reflected back clearly or they will push, thereby creating a harsh, shrill, or possibly out of tune sound.

To break down this approach a bit more, let's continue thinking about how formant tuning works. We already know that treble voices, particularly, adjust their vowels to create more resonant focus and vocal freedom. These singers may not be focusing on the progression of the /i/ vowel to /I/, for instance, but they will recognize the need for more jaw release to free the sound. Changed voice male singers must employ a slightly different approach, as they retain their "chest" voices into their upper ranges. To achieve that mix, they must initially modify vowels (often using mixed vowels, like a German /ö/), until they move beyond the *passaggio*.

A more familiar term for this methodology is *cover*. In general, solo singers modify by singing "purer" vowels in their lower registers and more openly modified vowels in their upper registers. To do this, they not only think of the vowel they wish to produce, but they also consciously or unconsciously adjust their vocal tracts to achieve the desired vocal ring. Formant tuning is an acoustical explanation for resonance changes, whereas vowel modification is a more singer-friendly explanation of the same thing. Diction has to change as pitches change.

DICTION AND VOWEL MODIFICATION IN CHORAL SINGING

Choral singers have the added challenge of employing these resonance strategies while producing diction that is understandable as an ensemble. You now know that diction and resonance are strongly related. Diction needs to be as clear as possible with a pleasing timbre. Usually, choirs are populated with people from a particular geographic area for convenience, so they share a similar pronunciation. With the help of the conductor, the individual singers make slight modifications to satisfy the tonal ideal the conductor may have. If an international pronunciation of English (or any other language) is desired, then it is very helpful if both the conductor and the choir members know the International Phonetic Alphabet. This shorthand codification of language, which has been used in this chapter when naming vowels, helps unify diction. However, most choirs in the United States are not completely familiar with this tool, and it often becomes the conductor's job to help them create vowels that will work together rather than acoustically fight each other. Understanding both the need for vowel modification in higher pitches for all singers (especially for sopranos) and the role of vocal tract shaping to create vocal color and clarity of text is vital.

CHAPTER REFERENCES

Mitchell, S. *She Walks in Beauty.* New York: Bethany House (2010).

Sundberg, J. *The Acoustics of the Singing Voice* (1977).
        http://www.zainea.com/voices.htm

CHAPTER 3

GOOD VIBRATIONS:
VOCAL RESONANCE AS CHORAL RESONANCE

Kathy Kessler Price

It's terrible but you know I just love the sound of my own voice. Sometimes I simply move myself to tears. I suppose I must be my own best fan. I don't care if that sounds immodest—I feel that all singers must enjoy the sound they make if they're to have others enjoy it, too.

—Leontyne Price
Gramophone (1971)

We must and should enjoy the sounds of our own voices—both as soloists and as members of a collective voice. If not, where will we find the necessary energy and motivation to bring our voices to their full potential?

Choirs are composed of discrete singers whose voices are governed by acoustical principles. The acoustical laws that apply to individuals still hold true when they are singing with others. Each chorister seeks to sing his or her personal best while listening and making the "whole" work. A primary difference, of course, between solo and choral singing is that the solo singer is entirely responsible for creating resonant, articulated sounds that carry in a space, while the choral singer shares that responsibility with others. Further, the soloist chooses his or her preferred expressive colors and dynamics, whereas choristers seek to fulfill a shared vision, guided by the conductor. Solo singers also have a better chance to hear their voices reverberate within the room, while choristers have to hear themselves in the midst of others. It is this last point that is the focus of this chapter.

How do we find the balance in singing between our own voices and those of our fellow choristers?

SELF TO OTHER

Ternström (1999, 1995, 1994), a music acoustics researcher at the Royal Institute of Technology in Sweden, has coined a phrase called *"Self-to-Other Ratio" (SOR)*. It is just what it sounds like—we balance listening to ourselves while listening to those around us. "Other" refers to the rest of the choir (usually experienced most strongly from the voices of the people immediately around us) and the reverberation of the total choral sound in the room. If that ratio is too weighted on one side or the other, there's trouble. In general, choral singers prefer to hear themselves more distinctly than their neighbors, but they want to hear their neighbors, too.

When we cannot hear ourselves sufficiently, we push a bit, press the tone, change the breath pressure, etc., to increase our self-perception. Unfortunately, that very straining is not only vocally stressful, but it can also affect intonation and timbre in detrimental ways. This phenomenon has a name: the *Lombard Effect*. It is the tendency to raise one's voice in an environment where it is hard to hear. The effect applies whether we are speaking or singing. Imagine yourself in a noisy restaurant trying to talk to someone across the table. By the end of the dinner, you are vocally exhausted and wonder why. The recent trend toward exposed brick, lofted ceilings with exposed pipes, and hard-floor surfaces in many restaurants contribute to this vocal fatigue. Waiters are in the most jeopardy, and they are often singers and actors making a livelihood as voice professionals.

Ternström (1994) indicated that there were two major, acoustical factors for choristers that control the SOR. First, Ternström suggested the amount of space between and among the choristers could be altered, changing what the individual chorister hears from those directly around him or her. Ternström's studies have indicated the decibel level choristers prefer varies from 3 to 6+ in favor of hearing oneself over others through the auditory feedback loop. Second, the amount of reverberation in the performance/rehearsal space coming primarily from the "Other" affects the SOR. The combination of the two (space between singers and room reverberation) are what comprise the "Other" for each chorister. Ternström suggested that the choral conductor may be able to control both factors.

AUDIENCE-LEVEL LISTENING

Many conductors may have differing views about the last statement, to a degree. Spacing may, indeed, be under the direct auspices of the conductor—at least to the point the performance space allows it (more on that in Chapter 6: Good Vibrations: Choral Spacing). However, the reverberation of the room may be a more difficult matter to know and accommodate. Though familiarity with the performance room reverberation is ideal, it is often not feasible to gain the acoustical information needed in time to affect changes in choral formation/ spacing prior to performance. Think of a "typical" choir tour: possibly arriving late on the bus, rushing in to find where the singers will stand, perhaps working through an interpreter if traveling abroad, and on and on. In these instances, it may feel like a bit of a miracle that the concert happens at all, is well received, and the singer/audience connection feels satisfied. The idea of being able to gain acoustical information on reverberation and audibility of text before the concert is a bridge too far.

When possible, however, this knowledge and the time it takes to achieve it can be critical to choral success. Too often acoustical matters are not considered seriously enough before a performance, when a modicum of advance planning could make all the difference. In a first rehearsal in a new venue, choral conductors feel pushed to rehearse the orchestra (often the only rehearsal with the instrumentalists) as well as the chorus in a truncated time, and handle all the logistics of the choir's participation in an unfamiliar space. However, the simple addition of placing an expert, trusted listener in the hall to give the conductor feedback during even a brief rehearsal can make a real difference. Since singers are working primarily on sensory awareness to sing well, and conductors are depending largely on their ears to assess the sound levels, but are not out in the hall, it is essential that someone at the audience level be enlisted to provide that third component—the ears of the audience. After all, we offer our gifts of music to others and not just ourselves. What a pity to rehearse for weeks for an event only to be defeated by a venue's acoustics!

An interesting sidebar to this discussion has to do with audible vocal resonance measured from the singers' positions to the conductor, and from the singers to the audience. Morris, et al. (2006) showed a 3- to 5-dB difference in individual harmonics among singers as obtained from the singer-position microphones. These decibel differences dissipated as the choir's sound reached the audience position, not becoming a factor in the listeners' perceptions of the choral sound. However, Morris suggested that the conductor might hear those singers' decibel differences as well and overly adjust for them when making decisions about choir formation. Clearly, it is advisable to have trusted listeners in the audience position during a dress rehearsal to help the conductor adjust to the acoustics.

HEARING AND SENSING

In the previous chapter, I alluded to singers relying on bone conduction and sensation for their primary feedback as well as the auditory feedback loop as they listen to their voices in an acoustical space. It is time to explain these concepts a bit further. Though we rely on our ears extensively as singers, the reality is that we do not hear ourselves as others hear us. The simple fact that we often recoil when we hear our own voices played back on recordings tells us there is something odd at play. Indeed, we hear our own voices through *forced resonance*—the internal vibrations of bone conduction traveling from our larynges to our pharynges to our ears and brain. This immediate and strong source of sensation and sound is how we judge our own voices, first and foremost. Second, we hear our own voices through the auditory feedback loop. In other words, we do hear our own voices as they travel throughout the space into which we are singing and subsequently back to us. Through this means we verify that we did what we intended, or we realize that minute changes are in order. The primary way we "tune" our voices is to tweak intonation and loudness, as well as clean up diction and make fine adjustments to timbre. That is a lot! Additionally, we have made many physical fine tunings based on sensation before we even hear our sound return to our ears. It is an amazing process.

Others, however, hear us entirely (or nearly so) through *free resonance*, or sound waves traveling through space. All of the minute noises, clicks, phlegmy sounds, etc., that plague us are not usually a part of what others hear or process, thankfully. They are depending on vibrations in the air tickling their ears and sending signals to their brains to interpret our vocal output as singing. It seems to me that this difference between a singer's awareness of self and a listener's awareness of others' sound is important. As the singer, we have *two* ways to adjust our singing: (1) internal bone conduction (sensing) and (2) sound waves in the air (hearing). We must remember to rely more on sensing than hearing when making those adjustments since that is the primary way we hear ourselves.

Choral singing is a slightly different beast from solo singing in this regard, however. We are not only listening to ourselves (or ourselves with instruments), but to other singers as well. The auditory feedback loop is in play to the max. Choral singers, however, must not lose themselves to this phenomenon. Sensation is still the name of the game in terms of vocal production and vocal health. Singers must rely on that, or they will find themselves over-manipulating and exhausting their voices unduly.

THE VENUE

In addition to singers performing individually and corporately and making constant small adjustments to their vocal production, there is another huge factor to consider: the performance space. Choral directors and their singers are often hindered by the limitations of space in each venue. Proper spacing for the best Self-to-Other Ratio may appear to be impossible with choir lofts into which singers are stuffed, risers that limit personal space, and the performance practice of placing the orchestra in front of the choir. However, as a later chapter reveals (see Chapter 6: Good Vibrations: Choral Spacing), room acoustics and choral spacing have a great deal to do with how singers perform and what the audience perceives. Choral directors would do well to be creative as to how they use the space.

At the beginning of the previous chapter, I mentioned the requirements needed for choirs to be sufficiently heard by audiences to bring their art to fruition. Vocal resonance has been discussed in terms of the individual singer alone and with others. How we listen to ourselves and to others is a critical component to singing quality, and how we discern our sounds is also, in part, determined by the venue itself. In Chapter 6: Good Vibrations: Choral Spacing, I will present research done in choral spacing, specifically, and offer some food for thought regarding the effects of this spacing on choral sound.

CHAPTER REFERENCES

Morris, R., A. Mustafa, C. R. McCrea, L. Fowler, and C. Aspaas. Acoustic analysis of the interaction of choral arrangements, musical selection, and microphone location. *Journal of Voice*, 21(5) (2007): 568–575.
Price, L. Leontyne Price speaks to Alan Blyth. *Gramophone* (August 1971). http://www.gramophone.co.uk/feature/an-interview-with-leon-tyne-price

Ternström, S. (1999). Preferred self-to-other ratios in choir singing. *Journal of the Acoustical Society of America*, 105 (6) (1999): 3563–3574.

———. Self-to-other ratios measured in choral performance. *In Proceedings of the 15th International Congress on Acoustics*, ICA 95, Trondheim, Norway. Vol. II (June 1995): 681–684.

———. Hearing myself with others: Sound levels in choral performance measured with separation of one's own voice from the rest of the choir. *Journal of Voice*, 8 (4) (1994): 293–302.

CHAPTER 4
APPLYING RESONANCE

Sean McCarther

The previous chapters introduced some of the foundational concepts of resonance and how they relate to the choral environment. This chapter will expand upon those concepts, discussing how these scientific principles can inform the work conductors do with their ensembles. As with Chapter 1: The Anatomy of Breathing, this chapter will offer numerous exercises, images, and metaphors to help promote positive change in your singers and your choirs.

But before we dive into changing sound, let's revisit and expand upon a few of the principles covered previously.

HARMONICS AND FORMANTS IN A NUTSHELL

As has been discussed, the vocal folds produce a complex sound wave rich in harmonics. As this sound wave passes through the resonators, certain harmonics are boosted, while others are dampened. The resulting sound contains peaks and valleys of acoustic energy (*see Figure 4.1*). Sound waves with a lot of acoustic energy in the higher harmonics are bright and ringing. Sound waves with a lot of acoustic energy in the lower harmonics are warm and round. However, if a sound wave has too much energy in the upper harmonics, we perceive it as too bright, harsh, edgy, strident, pinched, etc. If a sound wave has too much energy in the lower harmonics, we perceive it as too dark, woofy, manufactured, etc. Singers and teachers strive for a balance between the brights and the darks. This is often called *chiaroscuro*.

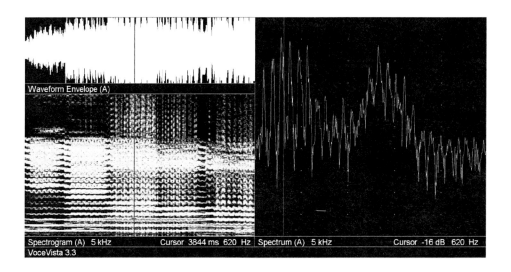

Figure 4.1. Example of Voce Vista display.
Vowels [i], [E], [a], [o], and [u] sung on pitch G3. The Waveform Envelope (upper left) gives a rough indication of sound pressure level within the audio signal. The Spectrogram (bottom left) displays time left-right, frequency top-bottom, and intensity via color. The Power Spectrum (right) shows one moment in time. It displays frequency left-right and amplitude top-bottom. The peaks and valleys of acoustic energy (evident in both the Spectrogram and the Power Spectrum) are indicative of various vowels.

Also mentioned in Chapter 2 was the term *formant*. A formant is a band of resonance, or a place of potential resonance, within the vocal tract. I often use the image of a bathroom to help my students understand this concept. If you have ever sung in the shower, you know that there is one note that makes the walls of the entire bathroom seem to shake. You have found the natural resonance (or formant) of the bathroom. If you sing a pitch other than that "special" pitch, you will not get the same result. The voice is similar in that there are certain frequency bands the vocal tract likes more than others. Frequencies that fall within that band get a boost, while those farther away from that band do not.

Another metaphor I use to describe this is that of a spotlight. If actors were to spread out on a stage, those who happen to be closest to the spotlight would get a lot of light. Those who are farther away would get less light. In this metaphor, the spotlight is the formant and the actors are the harmonics in the source sound. As a harmonic passes near a formant, it gets a boost. The closer to the formant the harmonic lies, the more of a boost it will get.

Unfortunately for those of us who enjoy singing in the shower, we only get one, maybe two, notes of super-resonant glory. If you want to change the resonant frequency of the bathroom, you would have to change its size, which is no small feat unless you happen to be handy with sheetrock and a tile saw. For singers, however, this does not require a contractor. Every time we change the position of our resonators (move the tongue, drop the jaw, round the lips, etc.), we change the size and shape of the filter. This moves the formant frequencies and alters which harmonics are boosted and which are diminished.

As mentioned in Chapter 2, there are five formant frequencies of note in the human voice. Formant 1 (affiliated with the back of the throat and labeled F1) and Formant 2 (affiliated with the front of the mouth and labeled F2) define vowels.[8] Formants 3, 4, and 5 all cluster around 3000 Hertz (Hz) and are responsible for the characteristic ring in classical voices. By modifying the formants, singers are able to balance the resonance system in such a way as to produce clear vowels with the most resonant tone.

ADJUSTING FORMANT FREQUENCIES

There are three main ways to adjust the resonators. Each adjustment alters the formant frequencies of the voice (primarily F1 and F2) and changes which harmonics get a boost and which do not. As the formants move, we perceive a change in vowels and/or timbre. These adjustments are:

1. **Size** – Making a resonance space larger lowers formant frequencies and encourages lower harmonics in the spectrum. Making a resonance space smaller raises formant frequencies and encourages higher harmonics in the spectrum. Since sounds with more acoustic energy in the higher harmonics are brighter, we can state that smaller resonance spaces tend to produce brighter sounds. The inverse is also true: larger resonance spaces tend to produce darker sounds. For instance, when one drops the jaw, the space inside the resonators increases and formant frequencies drop. Conversely, when the back of the throat is tight, the overall resonance space is smaller, and formant frequencies rise.

---

8   Though this is a simplified explanation of the rather complex acoustic system, it serves as a more easily digestible model for making practical changes in the voice. For more detailed information on formants, readers are encouraged to read Chapter 4 in *Resonance in Singing* by Donald Miller..

2. **Length** – Longer resonance spaces lower formant frequencies, encouraging lower harmonics, and shorter resonance spaces raise formant frequencies, encouraging higher harmonics. As with size, this has implications on the resulting sound. Shorter vocal tracts tend to produce brighter sounds. Longer vocal tracts tend to produce darker sounds. For instance, as the larynx rises, the length of the vocal tract shortens and formant frequencies rise. This produces a brighter sound. As one extends the lips, the length of the vocal tract increases and formant frequencies lower. This produces a darker sound. It is for this reason that most classical singers prefer a slightly lowered laryngeal position.

3. **Opening** – A narrower mouth opening (such as rounding the lips) will lower formant frequencies, and a wider mouth opening (such as spreading the lips) will raise formant frequencies. Thus, rounding the lips tends to produce a darker sound, and spreading the lips tends to produce a brighter sound. This is, in part, because of a reciprocal relationship between the lips and the larynx. As the lips round, the larynx tends to lower (lengthening the vocal tract and lowering formant frequencies). As the lips spread, the larynx tends to rise (shortening the vocal tract and raising formant frequencies).

SUMMARY	
VOCAL TRACT SHAPE	RESULTING QUALITY
Longer Larger Rounded opening	Warmer, darker, richer sound (woofy and manufactured in the extreme)
Smaller Shorter Spread opening	Brighter, more ringing sound (edgy, tense, brassy in the extreme)

These three adjustments are often interrelated. As I tell my voice science students, "Nothing functions in isolation." A change in one system will inevitably create a change (not always a desirable one) in another. Therefore, if I were to round my lips, narrowing the opening, I would also lengthen the vocal tract since the now rounded lips protrude slightly away from the teeth. Both of these actions lower formant frequencies and produce a darker sound. Similarly, raising the larynx often closes the muscles of the throat. This shortens the length of the vocal tract and reduces its size, raising formant frequencies and creating a brighter sound. It should also be noted that as the larynx rises and the muscles of the throat contract, the vocal folds themselves might start to squeeze together in a less-than-ideal manner. This will lead to a less harmonically rich and, thus, less resonant sound with increased vocal effort.

Remember that the goal of working with resonance is to create a *balanced* sound that is rich in low, middle, and high frequencies. A sound with all high frequencies would be akin to an orchestra with only violins. Conversely, a sound with only low frequencies would be akin to an orchestra with only double basses and cellos. Finding the right mix of frequencies within the sung sound results in *chiaroscuro*.

GOLA APERTA AND THE SWALLOWING REFLEX

The body is hardwired to protect the airway. Though it is fortunate that the vocal folds are able to make communicative sounds (and beautiful ones at that), their primary, biological function is to keep foreign particles out of the lungs. We have all experienced this when a piece of food "goes down the wrong pipe." The vocal folds close tightly and a forced expulsion of air (a/k/a a cough) blows the food out of the airway and back into the mouth.

The muscles of the pharynx (back of the throat) are similarly not designed for producing resonant sounds, but rather to aid in swallowing. When one swallows, several groups of muscles narrow and raise the pharynx to channel food toward the esophagus and away from the trachea. At the same time, muscles above the larynx pull it upward and forward, and the vocal folds adduct tightly, protecting the airway. This "pharyngeal phase" of swallowing is an involuntary act necessary for sustaining life.

Unfortunately for singers, the biologically appropriate and necessary action of these muscles is not conducive for producing a free and balanced sound. The back of the throat constricts, the larynx elevates, and the vocal folds squeeze together tightly, setting up the conditions for a tight, tense, edgy, and brittle sound. Obviously, singers do not often try to sing while they are swallowing, but these muscular patterns are so ingrained that it is often difficult to inhibit them when singing. Even so, it is imperative that singers learn to relax the muscles of the pharynx and release the larynx prior to and during phonation, establishing what the Italians called *gola aperta*, or "open throat." Richard Miller gives this wonderful description of the *gola aperta* in his classic pedagogy text *Structure of Singing*:

> When one breathes deeply...there is a feeling of considerable openness in the nasopharynx [nasal passage], some in the oropharynx [back of the throat], and to some extent in the laryngopharynx [space directly above the larynx]. The position of the tongue does not alter (it will, if the breath is grabbed noisily), the jaw does not hang, the larynx is not radically depressed, and the velum is not rigidly raised. Although spatial relationships among the resonators now have changed from those of "normal speech," neither of the chief resonators (mouth and pharynx) has become subservient to the other in this coupling. Yet, there is a favorable arch to the fauces [pillars of the soft palate], the velum [soft palate] is raised, and the connecting channel between the resonators is open and free. The same sensation of openness can be experienced whether one breathes through the nose or through the mouth.[9]

A few key points from this description. First, *gola aperta* is directly related to inhalation. As was discussed in Chapter 1: The Anatomy of Breathing, the term *appoggio* is not only about breathing. Rather, the breath gesture unifies the entire technique: alignment, breath, phonation, resonance, and articulation.

Second, and related to the first, *gola aperta* applies to the entire vocal tract, not just the back of the throat. When one establishes *gola aperta*, the tongue, the larynx, the soft palate, the jaw, the back of the throat, and the vocal folds themselves all find an ideal position for optimal vocal production. Some pedagogues call this *pre-phonatory tuning* or *positioning*. During a performance, it is impossible for singers to think about all the myriad systems that must work in synergy to make an efficient sound. The mind simply lacks the computational power. Instead, singers should be taught to link all these systems to a single unifying gesture. Richard Miller and others in the Italian School advocate the breath as this unifying gesture.

---

9   Richard Miller, *Structure of Singing* (New York: Schirmer, 1996), 59.

Third, in *gola aperta*, "neither of the chief resonators (mouth and pharynx) has become subservient to the other."[10] Establishing an open throat is an integral part of creating balance in resonance. As was discussed previously, the pharynx is primarily responsible for Formant 1 and the mouth is primarily responsible for Formant 2. If, in the quest for a bright and ringing sound, one over-emphasizes strength in Formant 2, the pharynx becomes "subservient" to the mouth. The swallowing muscles constrict the pharynx and elevate the larynx. The result is, indeed, a bright sound, but one that lacks freedom, depth, efficiency, and stability.

Of course, the opposite also holds true. If, in the quest for a round, warm, and mature sound, one over-emphasizes strength in Formant 1, the mouth becomes "subservient" to the pharynx. Singers enter a yawning state, in which the walls of the pharynx over-expand, the larynx depresses, and the tongue retracts. The resulting sound will lack freedom, ring, flexibility, and will more than likely become "stuck" as it ascends in pitch.

ADDRESSING RESONANCE IN THE CHORAL ENVIRONMENT

All of this technical talk begs the question, "How can directors help their singers balance resonance in a choral setting?" As with all aspects of vocal technique, addressing resonance in a group setting is tricky. Very few cues, exercises, or images will apply to everybody, which generality runs the risk of misunderstanding. As a voice teacher, I encourage everybody to find a private instructor who can provide individualized guidance. That being said, there are some things directors can do to help singers find a balanced and resonant sound. Below is a generic "flowchart" that will assist in this pursuit:

1. **Establish good alignment and breathing habits.**
    As I tell my students, it doesn't matter how beautiful the lampshade is if the electricity is turned off; without electricity, there is no light. The resonators will resonate whatever sound the vocal folds send through them. That sound must be freely produced by the vocal folds and rich in harmonics if the resonators are to have any chance of producing a vibrant sound. This begins with breath. For more information on establishing good breathing habits, refer to Chapter 1: The Anatomy of Breathing.

---

10 Ibid.

2. **Find an open throat.**

   Helping singers find an open throat is an integral part of establishing resonance balancing. As you work through the following exercises, make sure singers are not over-compensating and distending the walls of the throat. In all of these exercises, encourage singers to pay attention to the sensations they create. They should not necessarily "try" to expand the pharynx. Rather, they should do the exercises to the best of their understanding and observe what happens. "Trying" too hard will distend the walls of the throat and cause the opposite problem.

   a. Pretend to smell a flower or another pleasant fragrance. Be sure the breath is slow and deep.

   b. Breathe through your nose with your mouth open. Imagine that the air is curling across the roof of your mouth. If air is taken in slowly enough, most people will experience a cooling sensation as the air hits either the hard or soft palate. Generally, singers should feel as if this spot gently lifts throughout the singing process. It might be useful to label it so you can quickly and efficiently remind singers about this through the rehearsal. I have used terms such as "arch," "dome," "butterfly arch," etc.

   c. Imagine as you inhale that a trapdoor opens on the roof of your mouth, allowing air and sound to move up behind your eyes. As you sing, continue to imagine your sound continuing to spin in that "attic" space. A caveat: Be sure the breath still stays grounded and does not become clavicular with this exercise.

VOCAL EXERCISES

In general, vocalises that begin with a nasal consonant ([n], [m], or [ŋ]) are useful for resonance balancing. Exercises 1.a and 1.b are good examples. Forward vowels (such as [i] and [e]) are helpful in encouraging brighter, more ringing sounds. Make sure singers maintain an open throat and do not close the jaw to produce these sounds. Back and neutral vowels (such as [a], [ɔ], and [o]) are helpful in encouraging rounder, warmer sounds. Make sure singers do not overly open the throat and depress the larynx in an attempt to sound darker or more mature.

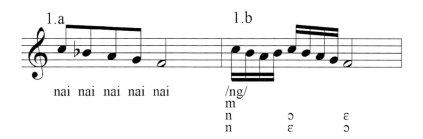

Exercises 1.a and 1.b

Often, pairing a forward vowel and a back vowel can be useful in helping singers find a balance between bright and dark. Exercises 2.a and 2.b are a few exercises that may be useful in establishing a balance between bright and dark qualities. Exercise 3 can help singers coordinate breath and tone.

Exercises 2.a and 2.b

Exercise 3

There are a few myths, misconceptions, or general faults that often accompany resonance. I would like to address the most common.

1. **Bright is always right** – Classical singers and teachers tend to gravitate toward brighter sounds. From a technical perspective, these kinds of sounds are generally more efficient, more flexible, and more able to carry over a large orchestra or in a large space. From an aesthetic perspective, these kinds of sounds are vibrant, youthful, exciting, and (at least in my opinion) more pleasant to listen to. However, just as "use more support" is not always the remedy for a less-than-efficient breathing system, "make it brighter" is not always the remedy for resonance. Remember that the goal is a balanced resonance system complete with high, middle, and low frequencies in the harmonic spectrum. Singers with bright voices created either by nature or by poor technique need to be guided toward a more balanced sound, not necessarily a brighter sound.

   Similarly, of equal importance to achieving a bright sound is the way in which that bright sound is created. Remember that to make a sound brighter, all one has to do is raise the formant frequencies. This can be done by spreading the lips, shortening the vocal tract, decreasing the size of the resonators, tension, or some combination of those. Remember also that the swallowing muscles are already biologically programmed to constrict. It has been my experience that singers (experienced and inexperienced) often will unconsciously resort to this swallowing reflex when asked to create a brighter sound. The result is a constricted pharynx, elevated larynx, and a brittle sound that lacks the vibrancy of a freely produced, balanced voice. Instead of brighter or darker, I typically ask my singers to modify their vowels toward a more forward vowel ([i], [I], [e], [E], or [ae]) for brighter sounds and toward a more rounded vowel ([ɔ], [o], [ʊ], or [u]) for darker sounds, always working to maintain an open throat regardless of the vowel being formed. Brilliance and ring in the sound is the result of balanced resonance, not the cause of it.

2. **Put it in the mask and placement** – Many singers are aware that
    the way they perceive their own sound is vastly different from
    how an audience perceives their sound. For this reason, singers
    are told to go by feel rather than sound. Some of the most typical
    resonance sensations are buzzy feelings in the nose, the roof of
    the mouth, on the lips, or behind the eyes. These sensations are so
    ubiquitous, in fact, that teachers of singing have coined the term
    "mask sensations" to describe them. So, it is not uncommon for
    singers to talk about "singing in the mask" in lieu of saying the
    more pedantic "vibratory sensations in the zygomatic region."

    As with many other areas of resonance, these "mask
    sensations" should be a result of balanced resonance—they are not
    the cause of it. When singers are over-zealous about "placing" the
    voice anywhere, it inevitably leads to tension. Rather than asking
    singers to place their voice, it is generally better to use some of
    the strategies above to help them find their own unique resonance
    balance. Each person will feel these sensations differently. It is
    much safer to allow singers to develop their own kinesthetic
    vocabulary rather than imposing one on them.

3. **Vowels are closed with the tongue or lips, not the throat** – Forward
    vowels ([i] or [e], for instance) are often characterized by their
    ringing and bright quality. If you recall from the previous sections,
    to create brighter sounds in the voice, we have to make the vocal
    tract smaller, shorter, widen the opening, or some combination of
    those. In forward vowels, the tongue arches forward in the mouth
    as the vowel closes, shrinking the space in the front of the mouth.
    As the tongue moves forward, the space in the back of the mouth
    opens and gets larger. Therefore, an [i] vowel is characterized by
    a large space in the back of the mouth (lowering F1) and a small
    space in the front of the mouth (raising F2). A spectrum of these
    vowels will show a low first formant and a high second formant
    (see Figure 4.2). The acoustic energy in the high second formant
    gives closed vowels their characteristic brilliance and ring.

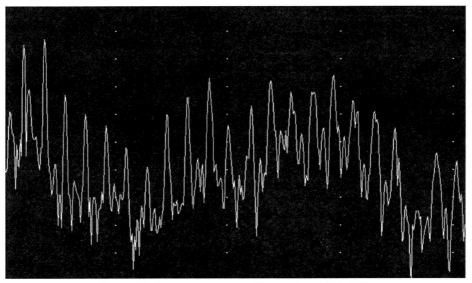

Figure 4.2. Power spectrum of [i] vowel on pitch F#3.
Dotted lines represent 1k Hz. The boosted harmonics at the bottom around 400 Hz
(F_1) and in the middle just below 2k Hz (F_2) give [i] its characteristic color. The boosted
harmonics around 3k Hz are a cluster of Formants 3, 4, and 5.

Similar to "Bright is always right," some singers will often achieve this brilliance through a tight throat and a high larynx rather than allowing the tongue to arch forward. It is not uncommon for me to see a student's tongue almost entirely flat in their mouth as they attempt to sing [i]. The issue is not one of resonance or even diction, but rather one of articulation. Unfortunately, many people assume it is an issue with resonance and ask students to front load the vowel with a nasal consonant or make the sound brighter, "pingier," or more "ugly." The diligent students, striving to make the correct sound, lower the soft palate, raise the larynx, and/or tighten the throat. The resulting sound, though potentially bright, will be nasal and lack freedom, ease, and depth.

Rather than addressing this via resonance, I advise addressing it via articulation. The singers need to release the tongue so it can move freely in the mouth and assume the high arched position associated with forward vowels without compromising the open throat. Asking singers to exaggerate the motion of the tongue in exercises—such as [ja ja ja ja ja]—so the middle portion of the tongue extends out of the mouth can help relieve tension in the base of the tongue and help establish new articulatory patterns. Other exercises incorporating sounds—such as [gala gala], [gala jala], [dɪgədi dagədi], or simply [nai nai] or [ne ne]—without the use of the jaw can also be quite helpful. Additional articulation exercises are included in Chapter 5: The Choral Warm-Up. Again, bright and ringing sounds are desirable unless they are created by constriction in the vocal mechanism.

4. **Training the singer's formant** – As a reminder, the singer's formant is a cluster of the third, fourth, and fifth formants and occurs around 3000Hz [Figure 3]. It is that characteristic ring, ping, or zing in a professionally trained voice that allows it to be heard unamplified over an orchestra. As such, it is an incredibly important part of a professional technique in the Western art tradition. Incidentally, it is also is present in many musical theater singers. It is thought that the space just above the vocal folds and beneath the epiglottis creates a small resonance cavity that enhances frequencies in this range. Essentially, singer's ring is created in the larynx itself.[11]

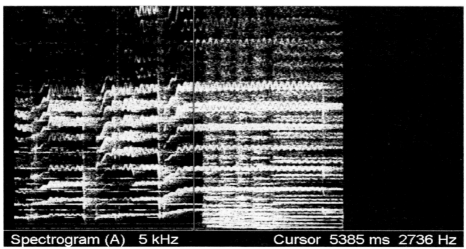

Figure 4.3. Spectrogram of Placido Domingo singingfinal note of "Celeste Aida," B♭4. *Color indicates intensity. Notice that the majority of the intensity of the sound occurs in the upper portion of the spectral envelope around 2700 Hz. This is "singer's ring."*[12]

11 For more information on singer's ring or singer's formant, see Sundberg (1987), Ware (1998), Titze (2000), or Miller (2008).
12 Adapted from Donald Gray Miller, *Resonance in Singing* (Princeton, NJ: Inside View Press, 2008).

It is difficult to affect the musculature of the larynx directly: you cannot ask students to contract their left lateral cricoarytenoid more firmly. We can use the swallowing reflex to elevate the larynx and the yawning reflex to lower it, but it is challenging to adjust the structure itself—and probably not that healthy to attempt to do so.

Instead of making the development of singer's ring a goal, I suggest we change our thought and allow this characteristic ring to be a result of good technique rather than the cause of it. If singers establish good alignment, open the body to allow an easy inhalation, use the inhaled air to set the vocal folds into free vibration, and achieve a balanced resonating system, including *gola aperta,* then they will achieve all the ring they will ever need in any situation. Attempting to manufacture ring by any means will only cause constriction.

CONCLUSION

As with Chapter 1: The Anatomy of Breathing, not all of the above exercises will be appropriate for every singer or group of singers. However, they should serve as a source of inspiration to the informed choir director. One of my favorite aspects of teaching singing is designing exercises, images, or metaphors on the spot to address a specific need in a specific singer. I encourage readers to do the same. Armed with a firm understanding of anatomy, physiology, and the basics of acoustics, directors should not be afraid to experiment with a variety of exercises. The goal is balance among the various systems and a free, vibrant, resonant sound that serves the communicative purpose of the music we perform. At the end of the day, communication is at the heart of what we, as musicians, do.

PART 2
TEACHING TO SUPPORT SINGING
AND LISTENING

CHAPTER 5
THE CHORAL WARM-UP

Sean McCarther

he way in which a rehearsal begins has a dramatic effect on the rest of the rehearsal. For those of us in education (grade school or higher education), choir is usually jammed into the middle of an incredibly busy schedule. Often, classes right before rehearsal have nothing to do with music, singing, or the creation of art. For those in non-academic environments, singers may be coming to rehearsal from work or family or a myriad of other activities. Regardless of the situation, the chances of your singers showing up to a 7:00 p.m. rehearsal mentally, physically, and vocally prepared to give their absolute best at exactly 7:00 p.m. is unlikely. For this reason, a systematic warm-up routine can be incredibly beneficial.

Though every warm-up should be tailored to the needs of the individual or the ensemble, all warm-ups generally share a common set of goals. Warm-ups should:

1. Focus the singers' minds;
2. Prepare the singers' bodies for the work ahead;
3. Re-establish good breathing habits;
4. Re-establish the relationship between flowing breath and a free tone; and
5. Awaken the entire range of the voice so it is fully prepared for the demands of the rehearsal.

How much teaching within each category you will need to do will depend on the skill set of your choir.

FOCUSING THE MIND

For many people, particularly outside of the academic environment, choir is a social event. It is a chance for people to get together with friends and make music. While this is, of course, a perfectly good reason to join a choir, it can be rather frustrating to the director whose desire for a high-quality performance is often sabotaged by idle chitchat.

This leaves directors in an awkward position. We do not want to squash the social aspect or the ensemble, but at the same time we need the singers to focus. The warm-up can be a great time to help singers transition from the social world outside the rehearsal to the focused attention necessary to make great music. Following are a few thoughts on how to make this transition:

1. Plan the warm-up to include activities that will allow the choir a chance to socialize. Instead of rushing into nine-note scales, messa di voce, and range extension exercises, start with some simple bodywork exercises that will allow the singers a chance to get the chitchat done at the start of the rehearsal. It is healthier for the voice to stretch the body first anyway.

2. Begin with spoken rather than sung exercises. The mind does not focus instantly; rather, it needs to be "coaxed" into a focused state. By starting with spoken warm-ups, you can address vocal technique in a less formal setting and slowly start to gather the singers' attention.

3. Consider the use of chant after the warm-up exercises to heighten listening and breathing, and to create a sense of ensemble phrasing going into the rehearsal.

PREPARING THE BODY TO SING

Since singers will likely come to rehearsal having just spent most of their day behind a desk staring at a teacher or a computer screen, it is important to use the warm-up to help them re-establish free and efficient alignment and use of their bodies. This can take many different forms, but it should include some exercises to release tension, increase blood flow, and prepare the body to sing.

Some general stretching can be quite useful in opening up the body. Stretches should emphasize opening the chest and the abdomen, and releasing tension in the shoulders and neck. Shoulder rolls, shoulder shrugs, arm circles, head rolls, etc., are great ways to release tension. Shoulder massages are also a rather ubiquitous way to release tension.

The following stretching exercises are ideal to give more social singers a chance to catch up with the people around them while simultaneously preparing them to sing:

1. Extend arms out to the sides with palms up. Open the arms so the thumbs (now pointing behind the body) start to move gently back. This opens the chest and stretches the muscles in front of the shoulder.

2. Raise both hands over the head. Drop the left hand and then lean to the left, extending through the fingertips of the right hand. This will stretch the right side of the body. Only stretch as much as is comfortable. Repeat with the other side. Focus on the expansion of the area between the hip and lower ribcage of the stretched side. This will bring attention to the lower ribcage and abdomen, and start to remind singers about proper breathing for singing.

3. "The Monkey" (borrowed from Alexander technique) – Singers will need a bit of room for this one. Stand with the feet wider than the shoulders. The knees should be bent, the upper body should lean slightly forward, and the arms and shoulders should hang loosely. Begin to bounce up and down while rotating gently from side to side. The arms should hang limply, and as the torso rotates, they will swing gently side to side. This will help the lower abdominal muscles and the shoulder girdle to release. Focus awareness on the lower belly and release of the shoulders.

    In voice lessons, I often end the physical warm-up portion with this exercise. While doing the monkey, I lead students through some non-singing vocal exercises.

RE-ESTABLISHING BREATHING HABITS

Since the majority of singers in non-professional choirs may not have taken voice lessons before, it is a good idea to begin each rehearsal with a brief reminder or explanation of what it means to take a "singer's breath." This is covered in more detail in Chapter 1: The Anatomy of Breathing, but following are a couple ways to incorporate this information into a warm-up:

1. **Simple reminder** – The most straightforward way to promote great change in the way people sing may be to give a simple reminder of what physically happens during a singer's breath. Briefly remind singers that the sternum should stay high, the diaphragm should descend, and they should only feel expansion beneath the level of the sternum (i.e., not in the shoulders). Singers should work to keep the sternum and shoulders passive during breathing. (Resist the temptation to say, "If your shoulders are moving, you are doing it wrong.")

2. **Expansion into hands** – Place hands on the sides of the body, paying particular attention to the space between the hip and rib. Breathe in such a way that this space expands outward, into the hands.

3. **Fingers apart** – Similarly, place hands on the sides of the body beneath the ribcage so the thumbs point down and the fingers fan across the lower back and touch in the back. Breathe in such a way that the fingers slowly part during the inhalation. Work to keep the fingers apart during the sung phrase.

4. **Water balloon breath** – Imagine holding a water balloon in both hands. One hand holds the tie at the level of the sternum. The other hand supports the balloon from beneath. When the bottom hand releases the balloon, it drops downward. Ask the singers to inhale and allow the breath to drop in the same manner as the water balloon. Be sure the singers maintain an elevated sternum during this exercise.

5. **Ping-pong ball at the base of the spine** – Imagine that a ping-pong ball sits at the base of the spine (sacrum). Inhale as if the ping-

pong ball could be filled with air. This might be particularly useful in a sitting posture.

6. **Panting like a dog (strike bouncing epigastrium)** – Have singers place their hands on the epigastrium (soft space directly beneath the sternum). Have the singers pant like a dog. The epigastrium should bounce slightly with each breath.

7. **"Butterfly arch"** – Ask the singers to take a slow breath in through the nose with the mouth open. Ask them to feel as if the air curls across the roof of the mouth as they inhale. In many cases, singers will notice that the air cools as it enters the mouth. Barbara Doscher called this the "butterfly arch." Singers should work to keep the butterfly arch raised during singing.

8. **Hissing** – Use a hissing sound to establish airflow. Have the singers experiment with both a high-pitched (high pressure) and a low-pitched (low pressure) hiss. Focus should be on maintaining an even airstream without surges and keeping the chest from collapsing.

PRODUCING A FREE TONE

As singers move from preparatory exercises to actual singing, it is important to relate everything to their speaking voices. Singers often think that their singing voice and their speaking voice are separate and require different techniques. The two are actually one and the same instrument. Humans produce vocal sound in only one way: air moves through the vocal folds, causing them to vibrate. This vibration creates a source sound wave that, when passed through the resonators, is shaped into all vocal sound, including speech, "classical" singing, belting, pop, rock, blues, etc. Getting singers to relate their singing voice to their supported speaking voice is often a great way to simplify the singing process and help them produce clear, resonant, and easy sounds.

If time allows or if you are looking for a fun way to change up your choir's warm-ups, try some of these speaking exercises. They can easily be integrated into many of the physical warm-ups listed above. Of course, many of the time-honored vocalises listed below are also quite effective.

SPEAKING EXERCISES

For the following speaking exercises to be effective, singers first must find a neutral alignment and use appropriate breath flow. Encourage singers to maintain evenness and ease in the exercises. This is a great time to remind them about legato, clear and resonant consonants, and articulatory freedom.

1. **Closed-mouth conversations**[13] – With a partner or by yourself, have a conversation using only the closed-mouth sounds /m-hum/ (an affirmative sound) and /um-um/ (a negative sound). Use these sounds primarily to explore the middle register.

2. **Umming and chewing**[14] – Perform the same exercises as above, but add a chewing motion in the jaw. Begin to explore the entire vocal range.

3. **Sirens and glides** – Continue the conversation using sirens and glides on lip trills, tongue trills, and raspberries.

4. **Unvoiced to voiced onsets** – Begin by hissing [s]. Establish a consistent airflow on the unvoiced consonant. Once established, slowly add voicing, changing the [s] to [z]. There should be no jolt as the singers make the change.

5. **Imitation** – Lead the choir through a series of vocal imitations. The goal is to get the choir to 1) have fun and 2) experiment with their voices. Be sure to explore multiple vowels, various onset combinations, and a wide range.

6. **Chanting** – There are several sentences you can use to help singers establish good breath/voice relationship and to help balance resonance. Focus on ease of vocal production, resonance vowels, and vibrant, free consonants. For the following sentences, link all onsets so there is no glottal attack. Chant freely in the middle of the voice and then begin to slide up and down.

---

13 Adapted from Maribeth Dayme and CoreSinging: http://www.coresinging.org/blog/vocal-warmups/
14 Ibid.

- Vira views violas.
- Neville needs knavery.
- His one lawn mower is noisy.
- Lions lying lazily in the zoo.
- Eeeny weeny kittens are meowing.
- Text from a piece for the next performance.

VOCALISES

There are many classic patterns that have been used for vocalises for hundreds of years. Triads, major scales, major arpeggios, and the like are staples in the voice studio. What I will discuss here are some variations on those ideas and the various vowel and consonant combinations that can be used to help coordinate the voice and breath and balance resonance.

1. **Onsets –** There is a reason that Richard Miller begins his classic pedagogy text *The Structure of Singing* with onsets. As he states, "The way a singer initiates vocal sound is crucial to the subsequent phrase."[15] Onset exercises are a great way to establish coordination between breath and tone. Exercises can be as simple as singing five quarter notes on [a] with a breath between each one (Exercise 1.a). Singers should work to have an easy, balance onset (a silent [h] without a glottal attack) and focus on the inhalation process. As singers become more adept with this, change the exercises from five quarter notes to nine eighth notes, still breathing between each note (Exercises 1.b and 1.c).

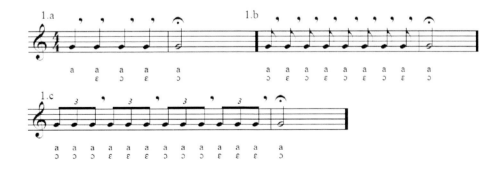

Exercises 1.a and 1.b and 1.c

---

15 Richard Miller, *The Structure of Singing* (New York: Schirmer, 1996), 1.

2. **Lip trills, tongue trills, and raspberries** – These are rather ubiquitous exercises that are fantastic for coordinating breath and tone. They can be used on triads, scales, or arpeggios. The vocalise patterns in Exercise 2 are some I use frequently.

Exercise 2

3. **Semi-occluded vocal tract** – Semi-occluded vocal tract exercises partially close the exit to the vocal tract. This occurs whenever a singer closes the mouth or forms a consonant. The more occluded the vocal tract, the smaller the exit for the air. As the air's exit gets smaller, the amount of pressure that builds up inside the vocal tract increases. As pressure above the vocal folds increases, it begins to equalize with the pressure beneath the vocal folds. Often, this will allow the vocal folds to release, creating freer phonation. These can be very useful in establishing breath balance and extending the range. Examples of vocal tract occlusion are:

- Humming and closing one nostril
- Singing into a straw
- Lip trills
- Singing with a hand over the mouth, almost completely closing off the exit

4. **Consonants** – Each consonant can have a different effect on the subsequent vocal line. Below are a few of the more useful and some related vocalises.

- **[s], [f], [θ], and other unvoiced consonants** – These unvoiced consonants can help establish airflow. Because these consonants are based more on airflow than air pressure, they can be useful for establishing airflow balance in the top. Be sure the consonant is freely produced, particularly as the voice ascends.

- **[z], [v], [ð], and other voice consonants** – These voiced consonants (like their unvoiced partners) can also help establish airflow. In general, voice consonants take more energy from the breathing mechanism. They might be more useful finding balance in the middle voice. Exercises 3.a, 3.b, and 3.c might be beneficial.

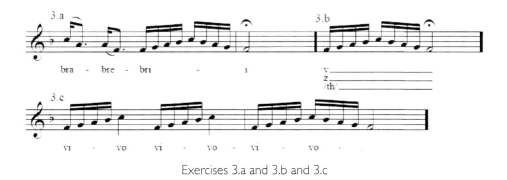

Exercises 3.a and 3.b and 3.c

- **[m], [n], [ŋ], and other nasal consonants** – Nasal consonants are very useful for establishing resonance balancing. They encourage forward, brighter sounds, which are usually beneficial to singers. Exercises 4.a, 4.b, and 4.c might be beneficial.

Exercises 4.a and 4.b and 4.c

EXTENDING THE VOICE

This last step works singers into the extremes of their range and works on developing more complex technical ability. For some choirs, this might be a relatively short portion of the warm-up; however, teaching untrained singers about the basics of registration and giving them practical solutions to navigate their higher notes is incredibly beneficial.

Notice that this comes at the very end of the warm-up. It is imperative that singers organize the middle of their voices *first,* and then move to the extremes. As with the previous section, the exercises below are not, in and of themselves, revolutionary. The patterns have been around for centuries. Rather, I have tried to provide insight into why each exercise is useful and provide conductors options for dealing with common issues.

1. **Arpeggios** – Arpeggios are useful because they help the voice naturally find its way through the registers. Moving through registers and higher pitches is much less difficult than sustaining them. Various vowel sequences can help singers naturally modify their vowels. Women will, generally, move toward more open and neutral vowels ([a], [ə], [ɔ]). Men, generally, will round or close the vowel ([E] to [e], [o] to [u]). (Exercises 5.a and 5.b)

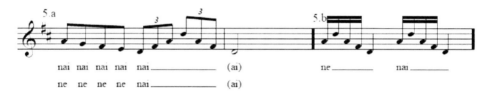

Exercises 5.a and 5.b

2. **Scales** – Scales work much the same as arpeggios, encouraging singers to sing through their register breaks rather than sustain in them. Again, vowel sequencing is key to success. Long scales with a large range are rather advanced exercises and should not be used with all singers. Use your best judgment. (Exercises 6.a and 6.b)

Exercises 6.a and 6.b

3. **Blending scales and arpeggios** – The air pressure required to sing a scale and sing an arpeggio is slightly different. Switching back and forth between them can help the breathing system learn to be flexible and buoyant, especially when you add articulation (such as staccato) to the exercises. These should be used with all vowels in all combinations. (Exercises 7.a and 7.b)

Exercises 7.a and 7.b

4. **Messa di voce** – Start soft, crescendo, and then diminuendo back to soft. Messa di voce is a fantastic way to teach breath flexibility and dynamic control, and it even addresses registration and vowel modification. These should be worked on all vowels. (Exercises 8.a and 8.b)

Exercises 8.a and 8.b

5. **Articulation** – Teaching singers to have crisp diction while maintaining free articulators is not always an easy task. Consonants are, by definition, a constriction in the airflow. Singers must learn to make that constriction with as much freedom and ease as possible while still maintaining the characteristic sound of the consonant. The following exercises will help singers find freedom in the tongue and jaw while still producing vibrant and resonant consonants. Exercise 9.a can be taken through the entire alphabet. (Exercises 9.a, 9.b, 9.c, and 9.d)

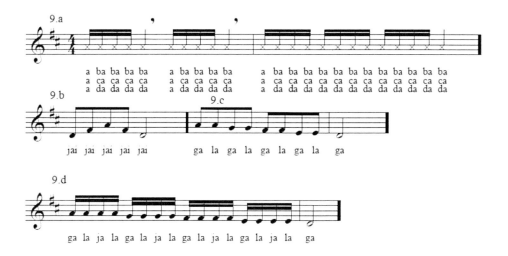

Exercises 9.a and 9.b and 9.c and 9.d

GOOD VIBRATIONS: CHORAL SPACING

Kathy Kessler Price

Lack of room is denial of life…(but) openness of space is affirmation of its potentiality.

—John Dewey (1859–1952)

A s choirs are composed of singers, the choral tone represents a shared understanding of vocal production, particularly the shaping of the vocal tract. For example, an English boys' choir would tend to employ head voice (a greater activation of the CT, cricothyroid muscle) with a corresponding longer and narrower vocal tract, whereas an American gospel choir would be more likely to use chest voice (greater activation of the TA, thyroarytenoid, muscle) with a shorter and wider vocal tract. The characteristic sound of the English boys' choir, then, would have a lot of loft and *"oo"* quality with an emphasis on the fundamental frequency. The gospel choir would sing with their more characteristic sound of strength and individuality with an emphasis on harmonic color. Most choirs exist somewhere between these two extremes and may choose to encourage different vocal coordinations for different styles of music.

The other factor in choral tone, acoustically, has to do with space—the room environment (dimensions, contents, etc.) and the space between singers. We often cannot control the former, but we can, to a degree, control the latter. To address the space and visibility issues, almost every choir at some point turns to risers.

RISERS

Since their invention, choirs have relied upon the use of risers to maximize space and sight lines. Risers were created to provide a necessary visual component: each singer in a group ostensibly can be seen and, more importantly, can see the conductor. In addition, early riser advertisements hailed risers as strong and portable—an early advertisement from 1943 (*see Figure 6.1*) shows many sturdy men with their weights listed below it (Daugherty, 2012).

Figure 6.1. Paysen's choir risers with many men to show the strength of the product.

Magnus Paysen (1875-unknown), a music educator, patented the first choral risers in 1930. They became the favorites of such famed choirs as the St. Olaf Choir (F. Melius Christiansen, founder in 1911 and conductor), especially as choir bus tours around the United States became popular. The risers could go on the bus and each new venue could resemble the previous one, accommodating the size of the choir.

Today, the use of risers is no less prevalent than years ago. The following advertisement was published on YouTube in 2012 for Wenger risers:

> "No other risers fold, roll, set up, or travel so smoothly. In fact, it's easy to take it around tight corners, across the parking lot, into a bus or a van. No wonder it's the #1 choral riser in the world."

The promotion of risers prioritizes convenience and portability, not a singer's ability to hear and be heard.

OTHER CHORAL SPACE ISSUES

In addition to risers, choir lofts, balconies, and other similar performance spaces are also limiting in creating options for spacing. In religious institutions, choir spaces have often been configured for theological or architectural reasons. Concert halls either have one flat stage or choral seating above the stage, which is often quite distant from a conductor or instrumentation with whom they are coordinating. Orchestras are placed in front of choirs, necessitating such a structure, or again, the use of risers.

SINGER AND CONDUCTOR PREFERENCES

Other factors that contribute to choral standings and spacing have to do with singer and conductor preferences. Many choral singers prefer to sing as a part of their section (soprano, alto, tenor, bass), and many conductors agree. Conductor cueing is certainly much easier with sectional standing orders. Others prefer to sing in mixed quartets or even in random order throughout the choir. Robert Shaw (1916–1999), famed conductor of the Robert Shaw Chorale, seemed to prefer a vertical dimension (rather than a horizontal one) to his choral standings, with quartets in vertical rows throughout the group. Social considerations (friends standing together) and singers' height, even with risers, frequently dictate who stands where.

Somewhat anecdotally, an internet response page following the Second International Physiology and Acoustics Conference in Denver, posted some comments and questions to a choral spacing study by Daugherty (National Center for Voice and Speech, 2004). One, in particular, came from Garyth Nair (1943–2013), a renowned voice pedagogue and researcher. He remarked thusly on his experience with conductor Robert Shaw:

> "The most extreme spacing I have experienced was with Robert Shaw, who liked to put us on a stage with 6 feet around each singer of space. That was so he could walk around and listen to us while we sang as a chorus. Some of us thought we sang better in that extreme position than closer together." (NCVS.org)

To follow that point further, Ternström (1989) stated that choristers receive more feedback from their own voices when emitting low frequencies rather than high. Imagine longer, slower wavelengths of lower frequencies moving around the mouth to the ear rather than the shorter, faster wavelengths of higher frequencies, which travel with more directional energy from the mouth to the far reaches of the performance space. Consider what this factor may indicate regarding singing in high tessituras and what it may mean for high voices in general.

STUDIES IN CHORAL SPACING
AND CHORAL FORMATION

James Daugherty, choral conductor, music educator, and voice researcher, has conducted research on choral formation (who stands next to whom), and especially on inter-singer spacing (the space between singers). In numerous studies (1999, 2003, 2005, 2011, 2012, 2013), Daugherty examined acoustical properties via *long-term average spectra (LTAS)* regarding tone quality of choirs to see if inter-singer spacing affected acoustical output and singer/conductor/audience perceptions. He identified *close spacing* and *spread spacing*.

Close spacing is the spacing that singers are accustomed to in many typical settings: shoulder to shoulder, with very little space between individuals who are contiguous (*see Figure 6.2*).

Figure 6.2. Close formation: A = Alto, S = Soprano, B = Bass, T = Tenor.
Photo credit: David Ross Lawn and Kate Miksits.

Spread spacing may be of two types: (1) lateral (*see Figure 6.3*) or (2) circumambient (Daugherty, 1999, *see Figure 6.4*).

Figure 6.3. Lateral spacing (12 inches apart, shoulder to shoulder):
A = Alto, S = Soprano, B = Bass, T = Tenor.
Photo credit: David Ross Lawn and Kate Miksits.

Figure 6.4. All parts in circumambient (24 inches apart, shoulder to shoulder, and 18 inches front to back): A = Alto, S = Soprano, T = Tenor, B = Bass.
Photo credit: David Ross Lawn and Kate Miksits.

According to Daugherty, both lateral and circumambient spacing call for 24 inches of space side to side between singers. However, circumambient spacing also includes 18 inches of space front to back between singers. Daugherty tested singers on risers, creating the front-to-back space by skipping a step and moving the risers back to allow the first row on the floor to stay in place in relation to the conductor and audience-placed microphones. He also tested singers in both sectional block and mixed formations. In each of his studies (1999, 2003, 2005) on mixed choirs, Daugherty found that spread singer spacing "influenced singer and auditor perceptions of choir sound more than the particular formation of the choir, [and] elicited significantly more in-tune singing regardless of formation." (Daugherty, 2015, p. 4). The reference in this quote to "particular formation" referred to sectional (SATB) or mixed formations.

Other studies (Daugherty, 2003; Ternström, 1999) also found that treble voices (and here we should include countertenors) appeared to need a greater Self-to-Other Ratio (as explained in Chapter 3) than lower-voiced men (tenors, baritones, basses) and, therefore, more inter-singer space. In other words, treble voices needed to hear themselves in the acoustic space more than their lower counterparts. The probable reason for this difference is the lower-voiced singers' access to the Singer's Formant. This resonant energy boost at the 2- to 4-kHz level is produced just above the vocal folds. Changed voice men, and perhaps lower voice women, experience this resonant boost because many of their harmonics occur in this frequency region. They "hear" their own sound internally through intense sensory perception. Since a higher, treble voice's upper harmonics (overtones) move more quickly out of the audible range due to their octave-higher fundamental frequency (base pitch), treble voices have a much harder time making use of this formant. Sopranos, especially, have high, more directional sound waves, so they need to hear more in-room feedback to adjust muscle/breath actions accordingly. Hence, sopranos, above all, need circumambient space to sing freely, beautifully, and in tune! All treble voices need more space around them than lower-voiced men, and tenors may need more than basses. Treble male voices (pre-changed and adult countertenors or male falsettists) should be treated the same as their female counterparts.

If circumambient spacing for all is not physically possible because of space limitations or conductor preferences, there are other effective formations to consider. One spacing option *(see Figure 6.5)* shows tenors and basses in close spacing, and sopranos and altos in lateral. This spacing option would be marginally better than close spacing for all. The higher the voice, the greater the need for space.

Figure 6.5. Tenors and basses in close spacing,
sopranos and altos in lateral spacing (12 inches apart):
A = Alto, S =Soprano, T = Tenor, B = Bass.
Photo credit: David Ross Lawn and Kate Miksits.

Another spacing option (*see Figure* 6.6) allows the tenors and basses lateral spacing, and the treble voices circumambient spacing—a better option, in this writer's opinion, than that in Figure 6.5.

Figure 6.6. Tenors and basses in lateral spacing (12 inches apart),
sopranos and altos in circumambient (24 inches, shoulder to shoulder,
and 18 inches front to back).
Photo credit: David Ross Lawn and Kate Miksits.

In terms of chorister positioning, it may be beneficial to place singers with more directional sound energy (sopranos and tenors) farther back in the choir (*see Figures 6.2–6.6*). Their sound travels quickly to the audience because of the higher, faster frequencies (sopranos faster than altos, tenors faster than basses). Due to their less-directional sound waves, altos and basses would benefit from being placed more toward the front of the choir.

From an acoustical perspective, choir directors would be advised to place low-voiced women (altos) in front of high-voiced women (sopranos) and low-voiced men (basses) in front of high-voiced men (tenors). Another option is shown below (*see Figure 6.7*).

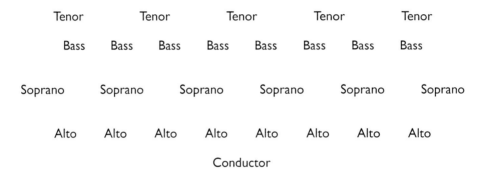

Figure 6.7. Choral spacing based on sound wave directionality and resonance strategies.

Note that there is more space between sopranos and between tenors, and less between members of the bass section and members of the alto section. There is also more space front to back for the sopranos—farther away from both the men behind and the altos in front. Obviously, the number of singers here is arbitrary and based on the space the page provides. Each choir has to adjust according to the size and numbers of individuals within a section.

Close spacing in Daugherty's studies brought self-reported body tension from choristers. "I tended to push or sing louder," a majority (85%, $n = 17$ of $N = 20$) of choristers responded, "when other singers were close," including 100% of sopranos and tenors (Daugherty, 2003, p. 54). Eighty percent of singers and 100% of female singers reported more body and vocal tension in close formation (typical riser stance).

One common argument against circumambient spacing is that it encourages singers to sing more like soloists, thus destroying the choir's "blend." Interestingly,

Daugherty, Manternach, and Brunkan (2011) found a significant *reduction* (2 to 4 dB SPL) of spectral energy in that very region of the Singer's Formant (2 to 4 kHz) when singers stood in a spread inter-singer spacing. The presence of Singer's Formant, that which gives a solo voice its ability to be heard more fully, even over an orchestra, is a frequently cited culprit in destroying choral blend. In the 2011 study, LTAS data showed that:

> ...regardless of riser unit, largely horizontal spread spacing (lateral, circumambient) of singers yields a consistent diffusion of certain higher frequency partials, notably in the 2.2 to 3.7 kHz region. While sound pressure naturally decays with increased distance from its source, these signal amplitude reductions occur while measuring the choir's sound at a consistent audience location. There is thus some assurance that differences stem from the independent variables of singer spacing and riser step heights. Second, choir members report that, when compared to close, shoulder-to-shoulder configurations, spread singer spacing is conducive to their most comfortable vocal production, better hearing of their own voices in relation to the sound of the rest of the choir, and better overall choir performance (p. 13).

Daugherty (2015) suggested that it may be possible to use "non-uniform chorister spacing (spacing that affords more distance between female singers and somewhat less distance between changed-voice male singers) without sacrificing and perhaps even enhancing characteristics of choir tone presently associated with uniform chorister spacing" (p. 19).

CONCLUSION

To return to where we began, singers love to sing with others, but they want and need to hear themselves first and foremost. When they do, they can use their full toolbox of vocal technique, making personal choices about their vocal production to help them sing their best. This freedom allows changed male voices to employ the Singer's Formant without affecting choral resonance unduly and allows treble singers to sing without "push" in an effort to hear themselves.

The individual singer has a responsibility to bring to the choral performance a well-developed and prepared instrument. Once the singer is ready, the key to finding vocal freedom in the choral setting appears to be appropriate choral spacing, tweaked to the acoustics of each particular performance space. When these components are in place, singers are free to be expressive. They are not distracted by discomfort, physically or vocally. They can hear well, and they can respond to the conductor's communications. Audiences relax and engage in the spirit of the performance, and the art of choral singing is at its best.

CHAPTER REFERENCES

Daugherty, J. F. *The Effects of Choir Formation and Singer Spacing on the Tone Quality of a TTBB Male Chorus.* Unpublished manuscript (2015).

———. *The effects of choir spacing and choir formation on the tuning accuracy and intonation tendencies of a mixed choir.* Paper presented at the Acoustical Society of America National Conference, Minneapolis, MN October 2005).

———. Choir spacing and formation: Choral sound preferences in random, synergistic, and gender-specific chamber choir placements. *International Journal of Research in Choral Singing, 1*(1) (2003): 48–59.

———. (1999). Spacing, formation, and choral sound: Preferences and perceptions of auditors and choristers. *Journal of Research in Music Education, 47*(3) (1999): 224–238.

Daugherty, J. F., J. N. Manternach, M. C. Brunkan. Portable choral riser units in three singer-spacing conditions. Acoustic and perceptual measures of SATB choir performances on two types of portable choral riser units in three singer-spacing. *International Journal of Music Education,* DOI: 10.1177/0255761411434499 (2012).

Daugherty, J. F., J. N. Manternach, R. C. Coffeen, and M. C. Brunkan. *Effects of two singer spacing condition and two riser step heights on acoustic and perceptual measure of choir sound acquired from conductor and audience position microphones.* Paper presented at the Voice Foundation Symposium, Philadelphia, PA (June 2011).

Dewey, J. (1934). *Art as experience.* New York: G. P. Pulnam's Sons (1934): 209.

CHAPTER 6
GOOD VIBRATIONS: CHORAL SPACING

Holt, M., and J. M. Jordan. *The School Choral Program: Philosophy, Planning, Organizing, and Teaching.* Chicago: GIA Publications (2008).

National Center for Voice and Speech (2004):
http://www.ncvs.org/pas/2004/pres/daugherty/daugherty.htm

Ternström, S. (1999). Preferred self-to-other ratios in choir singing. *Journal of the Acoustical Society of America*, *105*(6) (1999): 3563–3574.

Wenger Risers. Accessed March 19, 2015:
https://www.youtube.com/watch?v=KYHqYgXJ0Cs

CHAPTER 7

UNDERSTANDING LEGATO AS THE HEALTHY VEHICLE OF CHORAL EXPRESSION

James Jordan

Singers spend most of their lives learning how to sing legato. Singing, when it gets down to the most important expressive elements, is about legato. Yet, for some reason, choral conductors are reluctant to acknowledge the central role that true legato singing has in choral singing.

I have never really been sure where those of us who have been choral conductors for years acquired our understanding of legato—or rather, diction within a choral context. If you are like me, I always believed that diction, especially consonants, was the way to arrive at "clean" choral textures that align themselves in our thought processes to "good choral singing." Consonants are used in this sphere of thought as "sonic clarifiers." That is, when we sing quick consonants that spring to the vowel, we are singing "cleaner" and serving the vocalic flow of the singer's musical line. Much of our current thinking was formed in the United States over the past sixty years when voice science either didn't exist or when choral conductors did not pay it much due. Colleagues such as Scott McCoy, Kathy Price, Sean McCarther, and Christopher Arneson have opened my ears and mind to the very real reality of the necessary co-mingling of voice science and our pedagogy within the choral rehearsal.

Allow me to put forth the idea that the concept of legato is misunderstood by choral conductors. Much of our diversion has had to do with a misunderstanding of voice science, breath, resonance, vowel production. Many of our American (and perhaps European) understandings of diction are creating vocal stresses of various kinds for singers.

THE REAL INFLUENCE OF ROBERT SHAW

Many of us know about the choral rehearsal pedagogy surrounding the rehearsal technique known as "count-singing," as espoused by Robert Shaw for his entire life. For those of us who have used count-singing, or who worked with Mr. Shaw, we understand that count-singing, when performed non-legato and *piano*, is an efficient rehearsal technique for clarifying and unifying the attack of each pitch throughout the vertical texture of the ensemble. But few realize that whether purposeful or not, count-singing actually ensures some degree of legato singing within the choral ensemble by assigning (albeit subconsciously) a rhythmic length to consonants! I believe Shaw knew exactly what he was doing because of the work he did at the beginning of his career with Fred Waring and his system of "tone syllables."

CONSONANTS AS A LIFELINE
TO MUSICALITY AND VOCAL HEALTH

The reality of *choral* diction should be a shared reality with *solo* singing. That is, the consonant should not be shortened to attain textural clarity; rather, it should be used as THE vehicle for legato in a choral ensemble. If we examine the morphology of the shortened consonant, its short life spent accenting the beat structure coupled with an accrued rhythm weight works against everything that is considered by most of us to be musical. The shocking thing I realized is that when one allows time for longer and more expressive consonants, the choral texture actually becomes more precise, not less so! Thought of another way, lengthening consonants allows consonants to be perceived by any listener in any acoustic.

Consider this sobering fact. Bel Canto or legato singing is the essence of singing—using consonants to connect vowels and carry expressive textual elements. If a solo singer works so hard to master a true legato, why haven't choral conductors tried to understand that legato singing is not only healthy singing, but understandable singing. The movement of air is paramount to any degree of vocal health. To shorten consonants for the sake of clarity violently interferes the forward movement of air and traumatizes the vocal mechanism. In sonic reality, legato diction using prolonged consonant sounds actually makes the choral texture easier to hear. Sung consonants, I believe, allow the consonant enough time to sound so that, from the listener's perspective, the texture is actually cleaner, not less as we have always believed.

CONSONANTS CAN SABOTAGE MUSICAL LINE

There is another argument supporting the lengthening of consonants. When consonants are shortened in the name of "rhythmic clarity and precision," in addition to undermining breath flow and energy, consonants quickly articulated are usually accompanied by a violent change of tongue position and excess weight that is thrust into the following vowel. In most cases, these quickly articulated consonants slow the forward movement of sound and tend to add undue and unnecessary rhythmic stress onto the musical line. This rhythmic stress carried by the consonant undermines musical line and intonation problems.

THE "NEW" DICTION

Choral conductors need to support what is taught in every voice studio in the world! We need to adjust our concept of what legato singing is—and more importantly, what it isn't. Consonants are just as important to expression as vowels, and perhaps more so.

- Longer consonants help to ensure continuity of breath.
- Longer consonants allow for musical lines to be truly expressive.
- Longer consonants help to maintain appropriate tongue position to sustain healthy choral resonance.
- Longer consonants carry sound and support an ongoing breath stream.

Conductors must first hear what appropriately lengthened consonants sound like, and then they must tailor conducting gesture to reflect this newfound phenomenon!

ELIMINATING THE PHENOMENON OF "LIEDERWURST"[16] FROM CHORAL SINGING

One of the most serious hindrances to healthy choral singing is a prevalent problem that voice pedagogue Richard Miller humorously labeled "liederwurst"—the "sausaging" of notes (i.e., each and every note has an inherent crescendo/decrescendo) to make the music expressive. This not only constantly interrupts musical line, but it creates a world of vocal problems for

---

16 This term is borrowed from voice pedagogue Richard Miller.

singers, both melodic and harmonic. Eliminating such "sound sausages" will create beautiful legato line and allow for clear and beautiful declamation of the text that takes its rightful place over the underlying and organic rhythm pulse of the work being sung. An understanding of lengthening of consonants married with elimination of note "sausaging" will result in the most beautiful musical lines and choral sonorities.

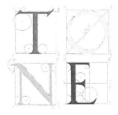

CHAPTER 8

VOWEL POSTURES AND CONSONANT EXECUTION: VOWEL AND DICTION CHALLENGES

Corey Everly[17]

Author's note: This chapter was written to illustrate diction issues contained in Eric Whitacre's *Lux Aurumque*. While the chapter is specific to that work, the vowel principles explained are central to discussions in this book and reinforce concepts presented in earlier chapters. This chapter is excerpted from the text *Inside the Choral Rehearsal: Method and Rehearsal Guide for Lux Aurumque* by Jason Vodicka and myself (GIA, 2016).

> *Lux,*
> *calida gravisque*
> *pura velut aurum*
> *et canunt angeli*
> *molliter modo natum.*

This short and simple Latin text requires only the seven pure vowels used in Italian diction, and yet, those pure sounds are often the hardest for a choir to sing in a unified fashion. A host of consonant issues are present. When listening for intonation and diction, one must realize that the two are certainly co-dependent. *The slightest differentiation in tongue or lip position can affect sectional sound, balance, and intonation.* It is important to note that there are no shortcuts that will bode well for your singers'

---

17 Corey Everly, conductor, vocal coach, and collaborative pianist, has been associated with James Jordan and his work with the Westminster Williamson Voices for six years. His gifts as a vocal and choral diction coach have been integrated into the pedagogies used by James Jordan in the teaching of the Westminster Williamson Voices.

vocal health. Sectional sound, balance, and intonation are at their prime when each singer is making his or her optimal vowel on the given pitch. However, the optimal vowel may not always seem apparent when the singer is within a section. The role of the conductor to facilitate this varies based on the level of the choir. Professional singers, for instance, would not need to be micromanaged on tongue and lip formations; however, a community or high school choir would. But when intonational issues occur in any level of ensemble, pedagogical reminders are in order. While there are many voice science discussions that could go on in dealing with vowels, formants, and the overtone series, that is not the goal of this chapter. This chapter is to serve as a guide to troubleshoot any problems you may be hearing related to production of vowels and diction specifically related to intonation and sectional sound. Suggestions made here are based on the phonation of pure vowels and are not to be used in cases of extreme range. (High or low pitches per each voice part are in the pitch ranges deemed "passaggio" for each voice part.)

For each vowel, I will go through the pitfalls that young or amateur singers are prone to and what you might hear; then I will list possible solutions. This type of listening is hard and requires you to be sympathetic to some degree with how the singer is producing the sound. Many of the points I make can also be seen visually, so it's important to *watch* how singers are making the sounds and function as their mirror. *However, emphasis must always be placed on the space inside, as a singer may appear to be doing everything correctly on the outside when, in reality, the internal spaces responsible for forming the vowel are incorrect.* Again, this is not an exhaustive list, but a starting point—a pedagogically potent starting point that will ensure that what is heard in audiation will be sounded accurately in the sung sound of the section. The lowest common denominator to keep in mind is that vowels carry pitch, so therefore, a compromised vowel results in a compromised pitch.

THE ANATOMY OF VOWELS

The teaching of vowels and vowel sounds has for a long time remained central to the choral art. After all, vowels carry pitch, and we are in constant search of the balance between sweetness in tuning and execution of beautiful language. Both are possible! However, a succinct way to get fact-based, voice science research to the choir has been missing.

After spending many years as an accompanist and singer in the studio of Lindsey Christiansen,[18] I have come to realize the importance of the position of the tongue and the internal shapes and postures of vowels. I saw many approaches to vowels and vowel modification in my time as a singer and pianist, but few enforced the correct position of the tongue and its role in forming vowels and consonants as Christiansen's teaching so clearly did. She constantly used anatomy books and visuals to show singers the inside view of what really happened when a vowel was formed in the pharynx and how the tongue plays a major role. So I began implementing in my ensemble teaching and the private studio a vowel chart (*see Figure 8.1*) that codifies the exact position of the tongue for each vowel. The immediate connection between the visual and kinesthetic awareness of how the vowels are formed cannot be denied. The original chart I found seemed a little overwhelming, as it included many sounds we do not use in English or the most commonly sung choral languages, so I simplified the chart to contain all vowel sounds used in Italian, German, English, French (minus nasals), and Latin.

VOWELS

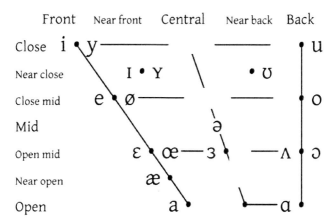

Vowels at right & left of bullets are rounded & unrounded.

Figure 8.1. Vowel chart.

---

18 Lindsey Christiansen (1947–2017) was Professor of Voice at Westminster Choir College. Her direct lineage to voice pedagogue Venard has been instrumental in the writings of this chapter and the teachings of this author.

GUIDELINES FOR USING THE VOWEL CHART

- The vowel chart[19] maps the position of the tongue for each vowel.

- When looking at the chart, you are looking at a side view of the position of the tongue, as illustrated below (*see Figure 8.2*).

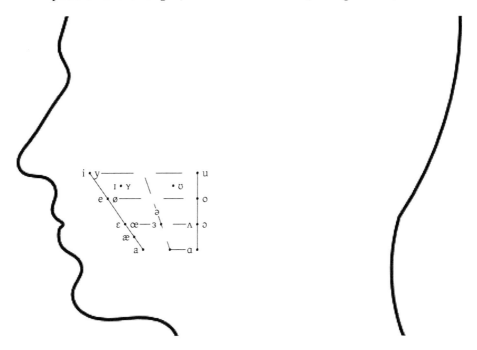

- Begin with [i] and [u] alone, and teach vowels in the order as they follow from [i] and [u]:

$$[i] – [e] – [\varepsilon] – [æ] – [a]$$
$$[u] – [o] – [ɔ] – [ɑ]$$

- Vowels to the right of the bullets are rounded.

- Vowels to the left of the bullets are unrounded.

- Notice the position of the schwa [ə].

- Open and closed refers to the position of the tongue from the roof of the mouth. It does not refer to whether or not the mouth/ jaw is open or closed, or the position of the lips!

---

19 The vowel chart shown here is an adaptation of the official International Phonetic Association's IPA vowel chart. For more information, visit www.internationalphoneticassociation.org.

THE [u] VOWEL
(Lux, pura, canunt, natum, aurum)

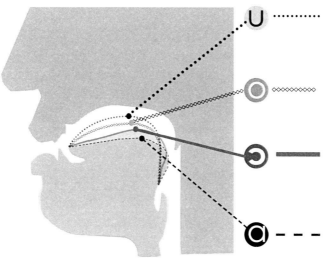

Figure 8.3. The [u] vowel.

The Pitfalls of [u]:

- Depressed tongue
- Lowered soft palate
- Jaw over-opened or tight
- Lips tight
- Lips spread
- Pulling the chin forward instead of raising the palate and the back of the tongue

The Correct [u]:

- Palate lifted (some singers feel the palate lift up and some feel it move back; both can be encouraged through pedagogical reminders (though typically the word "back" is preferably avoided when talking about sound)
- Back of the tongue at its highest position relative to other vowels (*see Figure 8.3*)
- Front of the tongue on the ridge behind the lower front teeth
- Jaw released down and back (a good gauge is to place one finger between the back molars)

Important Distinctions:

- [u] is labeled as a back, closed vowel, but it is not made by singing back and closed!
- The closure of the [u] is made by the back of the tongue, not by collapsing the space and pulling the lips forward.

Problems You Might Hear and Possible Solutions:

PROBLEMS YOU MAY HEAR	POSSIBLE SOLUTIONS
Sound is spread ("ew" as opposed to "oo")	– Have singers place a finger on each side of the cheeks between the back molars. – Have the singers place their index finger on their chin and say "i, e, a, o, u," without the chin protruding forward and paying attention to the tongue and lips.
Sound lacks color (proper resonance)	– Encourage that the back of the tongue is high and separate from the soft palate, which lifts **behind** the tongue. – Have the singers place their index finger on their chin and say "i, e, a, o, u" without the chin protruding forward and paying attention to the tongue and lips. – Have the singers pretend the vowel is underneath the tongue.
Sound is breathy	– Encourage that the back of the tongue is high and separate from the soft palate, which lifts **behind** the tongue. – Have the singers pretend that the vowel is underneath of the tongue. – Alternate [u] vowel with [i] encouraging proper change of tongue position, but consistent resonance. (The correct [u] vowel may certainly feel less resonant than [i] but should never be breathy.)

PROBLEMS YOU MAY HEAR	POSSIBLE SOLUTIONS
Men are in falsetto or not singing with coordinated registration/even resonance	– Use warm-ups that alternate front closed vowel [i] with back closed vowel [u] and encourage them to track the position of the tongue. Watch that the lips aren't engaged for the [i] vowel and that they are for the [u] vowel only, but emphasis should be made on tongue position. – Emphasize that the front of the tongue should be on the ridge behind the lower teeth, and that the back of the tongue doesn't make the pitches as ascending through passaggio.
Altos are singing in chest voice	– Have the singers monitor the chin with their finger while singing. If they feel the chin moving forward, ask them to make the vowel without the chin forward, emphasizing position of the tongue. – Have the singers pretend the vowel is underneath the tongue. – The [u] vowel by its very nature encourages head voice when properly aligned. Have them monitor the position of the tongue and lips, and do warm-ups that descend and require onset above the point of comfortable chest voice.
Singers are tight or easily fatigued	– Show a visual of the proper tongue position for [u]. – Have the singers monitor the chin with their finger while singing. – Have the singers pretend the vowel is underneath the tongue.
Pitch is flat	– Emphasize that the palate must lift behind the tongue in order for the resonance to be balanced and the larynx to be released. – Have the singers pretend that the vowel is underneath the tongue.

THE [a] VOWEL
(c̲a̲lid̲a̲, gr̲a̲visque, pur̲a̲, a̲urum, c̲a̲nunt, a̲ngeli, n̲a̲tum)

The Pitfalls of [a]:

- Tongue depressed
- Palate not raised
- Vowel really sounds more like "uh" especially at the end of a word (calida)
- Vowel spread
- Over-opened jaw (uh)
- Vowel not bright enough

The Correct [a]:

- Soft palate lifted (some singers feel the soft palate lift up and some feel it move back; both can be encouraged, though typically the word "back" is preferably avoided when talking about sound) – With [a], most singers will have the palate completely depressed, as it's more natural to say "uh" than "ah." They will certainly feel like they are working hard to find that same palate height on [a] than they may feel more naturally on [u] or [i].
- Tongue at a medial position in the mouth between the extremes—[u] and [i]—but *not* flat – A good way to find this position is by speaking from [i] to [a] slowly and sustained moving the tongue as little possible.
- Front of the tongue on the ridge behind the lower front teeth
- Jaw released down and back (a good gauge is to place one finger between the back molars)

Important Distinctions:

- The correct bright [a] vowel will be most difficult for American singers in particular, as the sound doesn't really exist in our language. Italian words (such as "mamma" and "amor") should be used as aural/oral reinforcement.
- At all times in rehearsal, the bright [a] must be reinforced even when diction is not being rehearsed or addressed. It is a new acoustical property as far as listening is concerned that must be learned.

Problems You Might Hear and Possible Solutions:

PROBLEMS YOU MAY HEAR	POSSIBLE SOLUTIONS
Sound is spread ("c*a*t" rather than "mamm*a*")	– Encourage "yawn" in the sound to reinforce the position of the soft palate. – Raise arms and place wrist of each hand underneath the cheek bones to encourage height of sound and release of jaw.
Sound lacks color (proper resonance)	– Place the thumb in the nook behind the upper front teeth to encourage aiming the sound in the direction of the hard palate. – Encourage that the front of the tongue is on the ridge behind the lower front teeth. – Encourage that the back on the tongue is not depressed. – Have the singers pretend the vowel is underneath the tongue
Pitch is out of tune (especially in middle voice)	– Raise arms and place wrist of each hand underneath the cheek bones to encourage height of sound and release of jaw. – Use warm-ups that alternate [i] and [a] to encourage that the [a] vowel is forward and bright. – Show visual reinforcement of tongue position. – Have the singers pretend the vowel is underneath the tongue.
More than one vowel heard (diphthong)	– Demonstrate the difference between the English words "size" and "fly" and how we often say the [aI] diphthong as one sound that isn't pure [a], as in the Italian word "mamma." – Have the singers place their index finger on their chin and say "i, e, a, o, u" without the chin protruding forward and paying attention to the tongue and lips.
Sound is too open ("uh" rather than "ah")	– Singers should place one thumb of space between their front teeth. – Encourage the difference between American [a] ("father") and bright Italian [a] ("mamma"). – Use warm-ups that alternate [i] and [a] to encourage that the [a] vowel is forward and bright.

THE [o] VOWEL
(m<u>o</u>lliter,[20] m<u>odo</u>)

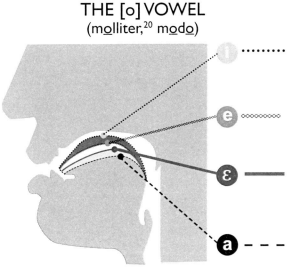

Figure 8.4 The [o] vowel.

The Pitfalls of [o]:

- A diphthong heard [ou]
- Tongue depressed
- Soft palate depressed
- Jaw over-opened

The Correct [o]:

- Palate lifted
- Tongue slightly lower than [u] but higher than open o or [a]
- Lips slightly more open than [u]
- Jaw has one finger of release between the back molars

Important Distinctions:

- [o] is found to be less problematic than the other pure vowels because there are no extremes. The tongue and lips are at medial positions relative to other vowels, therefore making it easier to make a balanced sound.
- Problems with [o] are generally caused by the consonants around it: the voiced [m] and [d], which tend to be formed under the pitch causing a "scooped" or out of tune [o] vowel.

---

20 This vowel is technically open o in IPA, but it is my strong suggestion that [o] be used instead for the purposes of tuning, especially in this piece, which is more about sounds than text. [o] encourages a slightly high tongue position than open o, better setting up the following [i] vowel.

Problems You Might Hear and Possible Solutions:

PROBLEMS YOU MAY HEAR	POSSIBLE SOLUTIONS
Diphthong [ou]	– Have the singers alternate between [o] and [u] feeling the micro shift in lip position. The diphthong will occur when that lip position is not monitored.
	– Use one finger on each side of the mouth between the back molars to encourage jaw release.
	– Emphasize that the tongue should be only slightly lower than on [u]; have the singers imagine the vowel is underneath the tongue.

THE [i] VOWEL
(calida, gravisque, angeli, molliter)

The Pitfalls of [i]:

- Tongue not on the ridge against lower teeth
- Tongue not high and forward
- Palate depressed
- Vowel over-darkened (rounding to fix problems, rounding instead of lifting the back of the tongue)
- Tongue position too low (sounds like "ih")
- Jaw tight

The Correct [i]:

- Palate lifted (with [i], it's good to encourage that the palate is also as wide as the back of tongue)
- Back of the tongue high and forward
- Front of the tongue on the ridge behind the lower front teeth
- Formed without the lips
- Jaw released down and back with one finger of space between molars

Important Distinctions:

- Don't underestimate the damages of over-rounding the [i] vowel. The danger is when the [i] vowel is rounded in place of the tongue being high and forward. While it is perfectly fine to round the [i] vowel, resulting in a mixed vowel, the pure vowel must be intact! Encourage tongue position first.

Problems You Might Hear and Possible Solutions:

PROBLEMS YOU MAY HEAR	POSSIBLE SOLUTIONS
"ih" vowel or mixed vowel (not a pure vowel)	— With the index finger placed on the chin, ask the singers to alternate speaking between [i] and [a] without the chin protruding forward and with an emphasis on tongue position. — Ask the singers to form the [i] vowel with the tongue high and forward, and to not pull down the lips. — Emphasize that the tongue forms the [i] vowel and the palate lifts independently behind the tongue. — Emphasize that the back of the tongue is wide and should touch the back molars. — Emphasize that the palate is as wide as the back of the tongue ("inner smile").
Vague or unclear pitch	— Alternate speaking or on a simple five-note ascending pattern vowels [i] and [u] encouraging same release of the jaw, but with the tongue and lips moving independently. — Encourage that the back of the tongue is wide and should touch the back molars. — Encourage that the palate is as wide as the back of the tongue ("inner smile"). — Ask the singers to form the [i] vowel with the tongue high and forward, and to not pull down the lips.
Color is not unified	— Use frontal voiced consonants (such as [z] and [v]) in place of text and/or in warm-ups to encourage the coordination of breath flow to sound. — Encourage that the palate is as wide as the back of the tongue ("inner smile"). — Ask the singers to form the [i] vowel with the tongue high and forward, and to not pull down the lips.

PROBLEMS YOU MAY HEAR	POSSIBLE SOLUTIONS
Hear individual singers (not a sectional sound)	– Encourage the singers to feel as though the vowel is underneath the tongue. – Use one finger on each side of the mouth placed between the back molars to encourage consistent release of the jaw. – Alternate speaking or on a simple five-note ascending pattern vowels [i] and [u] encouraging same release of the jaw, but with the tongue and lips moving independently. – Encourage that the palate is as wide as the back of the tongue ("inner smile").

THE [e] VOWEL
(gravisqu<u>e</u>, v<u>e</u>lut, ang<u>e</u>li, mollit<u>e</u>r)

The Pitfalls of [e]:

- Palate depressed
- Back of the tongue not high enough
- Front of the tongue not on the ridge behind the front lower teeth
- Jaw not released and chin comes forward

The Correct [e]:

- Palate lifted
- Back of the tongue high, only slightly lower than [i]
- Lips neutral
- Jaw released down and back

Important Distinctions:

- The tendency for this vowel to be either too spread or too tall is a challenge because we can't find a similar sound in American English. Therefore, careful attention must be paid to rehearsal technique in how the sound is spoken and aurally perceived.

Problems You Might Hear and Possible Solutions:

Problems you may hear	Possible Solutions
Vowel is spread (diphthong "ei")	— Have the singers say [i] [e] [ɛ] with one finger against the chin. Only the tongue moves! Have them observe the small distance traveled by the tongue. — Show a diagram of the tongue position. — Use warm-ups that alternate [i] [e] and [E]. — Use one finger on each side of the mouth placed between the back molars to encourage consistent release of the jaw.
Vowel not bright enough or too open (sounds like [E])	— Have the singers say [i] [e] [E] with one finger against the chin. Only the tongue moves! Have them observe the small distance traveled by the tongue. — Show a diagram of the tongue position. — Use warm-ups that alternate [i] [e] and [ɛ]. — Use one finger on each side of the mouth placed between the back molars to encourage consistent release of the jaw. — Alternate between [i] and [e] to feel the slight change of tongue position.
Sectional sound not agreeing	— Likely a culprit of varying tongue positions. — Alternate between [i] and [e] to feel the slight change of tongue position and encourage that [e] is closer to [i] than any other vowel. — Encourage that [e] is a tongue vowel and check to be sure no rounding is being done unless done by everyone! However, I strongly suggest pure vowels when not in extreme registers.

THE [ɛ] VOWEL
(<u>ET</u>)

The Pitfalls of [ɛ]:

- Palate depressed
- Back of the tongue not high enough
- Front of the tongue not on the ridge behind the front lower teeth

The Correct [ɛ]:

- Palate lifted
- Back of the tongue in a medial position relative to [i] and [u]
- Lips neutral
- Jaw released down and back

Important Distinctions:

- While it almost seemed silly to write about the [ɛ] vowel for one small conjunction ("et"), because the text "et canunt" is repeated a number of times, I thought it may be necessary. The openness of this vowel is up to the conductor. My preference is more like the Italian [ɛ] ("petto"), which is not as open as the American [ɛ] ("bet").

Problems You Might Hear and Possible Solutions:

PROBLEMS YOU MAY HEAR	POSSIBLE SOLUTIONS
Sectional sound not agreeing	– Narrow the vowel towards [e] by encouraging a slight shift in tongue position. – Have the singers say [i] [e] [ɛ] with one finger against the chin. Only the tongue moves! Have them observe the small distance traveled by the tongue. – Encourage that the Italianate [ɛ] is brighter than the American [ɛ]. – Reinforce in speech and warm-ups the brighter [ɛ].

PROBLEMS YOU MAY HEAR	POSSIBLE SOLUTIONS
Vowel is spread	– Encourage release of the jaw hinge by have the singers place one finger between the back molars. – Encourage the correct position of the tongue. – Encourage that the lips are neutral.
Pitch problems (typically flat)	– Encourage correct tongue position, especially with male singers, as the [ɛ] vowel can be wonderful if made correctly in the tenor voice, but it can also cause pitch problems if made incorrectly. – Encourage that the front of the tongue is against the ridge behind the lower front teeth. – Use warm-ups that alternate [i] [e] and [ɛ] to free the back of tongue and encourage proper resonance.

THE CONSONANTS

[l] . . . . . The American "l" is notorious for involving the back of the tongue. This puts pressure on the larynx and compromises the following vowel. Encourage that *only* the tip of the tongue makes the "l" and that the jaw does not shut. Encourage that the "l" is on the pitch and not below it. Encourage that the "l" is on the breath and vibrates (voiced consonants are sung). The first "l" should be formed through the position of [u] to ensure a beautiful first sound.

[k] . . . . The [k] is made with the back of the tongue on the upper back teeth. Do not close the jaw, or the following vowel is compromised.

Rolled [r] . I say "rolled [r]" because there is a phenomenon in which flipped r's are being made into the letter "d"—certainly not the same effect! Of course, I do not suggest an obnoxious rolled [r] in this gorgeous texture, but a flip should be one roll. The rolled [r] is useful in keeping the singers on the breath and usually will help the next vowel be of better quality as a result. The [r] must be on the pitch.

[v] . . . . The [v] is voiced! Make sure the singers are not doing the unvoiced equivalent [f]. I always ask singers to place their hand over their throat and alternate between [f] and [v], feeling the larynx vibrate when [v] is made correctly. Voiced consonants are so wonderful for keeping singers on the breath and the larynx free.

[n] . . . . Made with the jaw open only using the tip of the tongue. It is on the breath and vibrating, and made on the pitch.

[m] . . . . The image of eating a hot potato is helpful in creating an "m" with space behind; however, take care that the potato is the same shape as the vowel. In other words, a generic "uh" space defaulted to by most singers will be counterproductive. The space behind the "m" should be the space of the vowel.

PART 3
OVERVIEW OF THE PEDAGOGICAL PLANNING
OF THE CHORAL WARM-UP

CHAPTER 9

A MAP FOR COMMON GROUND
BETWEEN THE CHORAL REHEARSAL AND THE
AUDIATIONAL BREATH

James Jordan

Therefore, the basic trick is in the preparatory upbeat. It is exactly like breathing: the preparation is like an inhalation, and the music sounds like an exhalation. We all have to inhale in order to speak, for example; all verbal expression is exhaled. So it is with music: we inhale on the upbeat and sing out a phrase of music, then inhale again and breathe out the next phrase. A conductor who breathes with the music has gone far in acquiring a technique. (p. 272)

—Leonard Bernstein
in *The Conductor's Art*

One of the most influential tools in a conductor's rehearsal "arsenal" is the breath. For singers, breathing directly influences tempo, tone color, shape of phrase, ensemble dynamic, and spiritual content of the tone. For conductors, the breath not only affects the tone quality of the singers; it also affects what the singers perceive musically and all matters of interpretation and human connection. These factors are the wild cards, so to speak, in any rehearsal. A conductor who gains understanding of the breath and its impact upon the sound will gain one of the most valuable rehearsal tools.

THE CONDUCTOR'S BREATH

Stated simply, if the choir is to breathe, then the conductor must also breathe. As conductors, every choral entrance must be prepared by our own breath. We must be able to open our body to prepare for the breath to enter the body. This, perhaps, is the most difficult aspect of the act of inhalation. Many conductors confuse opening the body and inhalation, and as a result they combine both of the steps. The resultant breath is what I refer to as a "muppet" breath: the mouth opens, but air really doesn't enter the body, nor does it fall into a deep-seated location in the body. A muppet breath is characterized by the mouth opening at the moment of inhalation. If we properly take a breath, the mouth will open as a part of the breath preparation process. When inhalation is activated by the physical process of breathing, then air will simply and gently fall into the body. When done in this manner, the choir will breathe at the same moment, almost by instinct. These moments of breath should be the most magical points of any rehearsal or performance.

EIGHT-HANDED BREATHING: UNDERSTANDING INHALATION AND EXHALATION

I have found that the major factor that impedes proper inhalation and exhalation in both conductors and singers is a misconception as to how the breath works in an anatomical sense. I have found that one of the most valuable rehearsal techniques is to show and explain this breathing process using a technique called "Eight-Handed Breathing."[21]

Central to an understanding of the breath process is to have an understanding of what happens anatomically when breath comes into the body. When breath enters the body, what part of the body moves first, second, third, and fourth? If either the singers or the conductor does not understand this process, then neither will breathe well, and the tone of the choir will be adversely affected.

THE BODY MECHANICS OF INHALATION

During the inhalation process, the following parts of the body move in succession:

1. The **Ribs** of the back traverse or travel outward, with each rib traveling at its own rate.
2. The **Diaphragm** moves from a more-domed to a less-domed position.
3. The **Abdominal Walls** (front and sides) move outward.
4. The **Pelvic Floor** drops slightly.

---

21 A video version of eight-handed breathing to show to choirs or for conductor study and understanding is presented on the DVD *Evoking Sound: Body Mapping Principles and Basic Conducting Technique* by Heather Buchanan and James Jordan (GIA).

Note: Inhalation ALWAYS occurs in the above order with all of these parts of the body always participating!

Using the hands as a physical representation of the above, the sequence would look as follows:

Inhalation

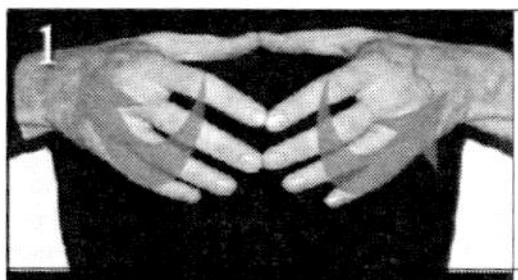 **1**	1. Ribs travel outward.
 **2**	2. Diaphragm moves from more domed to less domed.
 **3**	3. Abdominal walls move outward, both front and sides.
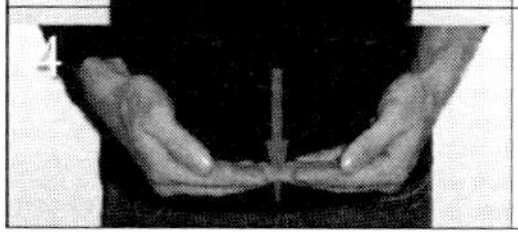 **4**	4. Pelvic floor drops slightly.

Figure 9.1. Eight-handed breathing technique – inhalation.

THE BODY MECHANICS OF EXHALATION

During the exhalation process, the following parts of the body move in succession:

1. The **Ribs** of the back traverse or travel inward, with each rib traveling at its own rate.
2. The **Diaphragm** moves from a less-domed to a more-domed position.
3. The **Abdominal Walls** (front and sides) move inward.
4. The **Pelvic Floor** raises slightly.

Note: It is important to understand that the ORDER of movement of the anatomy of the body is THE SAME for exhalation as it is for inhalation! Many conductors and singers believe that, anatomically, the exhalation process is the reverse of the inhalation process. This is a perceptual fantasy! Correction of this misnomer will dramatically improve the tone and expressivity of any ensemble.

Using the hands as a physical representation of the above, the sequence would look as follows:

Exhalation

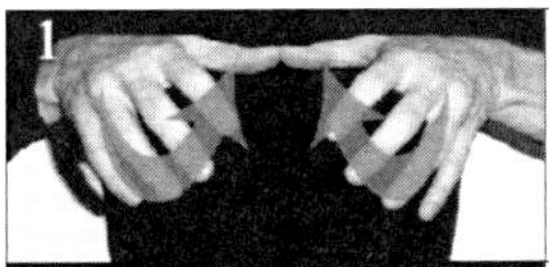	1. Ribs travel inward.
	2. Diaphragm moves from less domed to more domed.
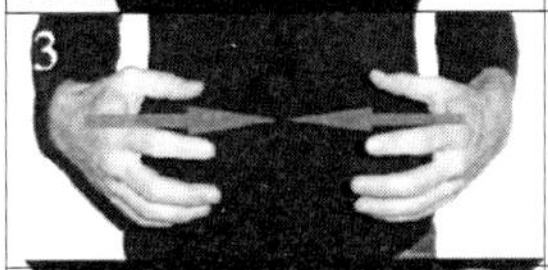	3. Abdominal walls move inward, both front and sides.
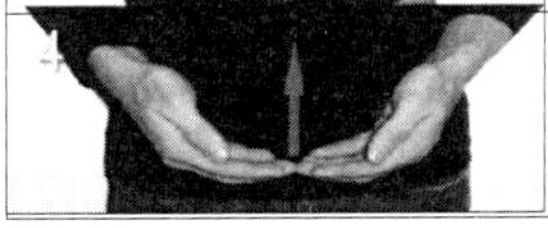	4. Pelvic floor raises slightly.

Figure 9.2. Eight-handed breathing technique – exhalation.

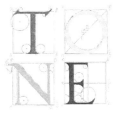

CHAPTER 10

THE CHORAL WARM-UP:
A PEDAGOGY WITHIN A SEQUENTIAL METHOD

James Jordan

Choral directors, even more so than teachers of singing, are divided in their opinions concerning vocal technique. Some refuse to employ any means to build voices. Either they consider such procedures to be unimportant, or they are afraid to use an exercise that is related to the singing process. Sometimes choral directors cloak their own ignorance of the singing mechanism by dealing directly with the interpretative elements in a score and, thus, avoid any approach to the vocal problems of any individuals in a chorus. There are those who insist upon using only the techniques of a favorite teacher. These are applied regardless of the nature of the problem or the desired solution. Finally, there are some who, without an orderly plan or procedure, utilize a great number of vocalises, devices, and methods taken from many sources with the desperate hope that the tone of their chorus somehow will show a marked improvement.

—Howard Swan
in *Choral Conducting Symposium*

Over the years, I have not encountered many exasperating experiences in teaching graduate students the "ins and outs" of the rehearsal process. However, it seems that all of my students struggle with basic organizational principles regarding the pedagogical construction of a choral warm-up. They have a wealth of exercises that they seemingly hurl at a choir without understanding that the pedagogical potency of any warm-up is buried in its unmovable pedagogical sequence. Of utmost importance is a realization that choral tone within each rehearsal must be nurtured and guided "to life" with a series of pedagogically sane sequences that reflect what any fine studio teacher would pursue.

IT'S ALL ABOUT THE "ORDER"

For years, I have relied on the pedagogical "ordering" of the warm-up that I learned from the legendary Frauke Haasemann. This intuitive teacher taught me that while we can never do everything a voice teacher can do in the private studio, there is a pedagogical "saneness" that we always must observe—the operative word here is *ALWAYS*.

Because I came into the musical world as a clarinetist, there is much I had to learn. Allow me to share how I learned about the "order" of things. Frauke Haasemann was my mentor and teacher. In the mid-1980s, we were making the VHS (now a DVD) entitled *Group Vocal Technique*. We followed Frauke Haasemann around the country filming workshops to gain material to demonstrate her teaching principles involved with what she called "Group Vocal Technique."[22] When we were finished recording, the final painstaking editing of the video was left to me. The process in those days involved a tape-splicing extravaganza, which for this project took me seven eight-hour days!

Prior to that experience, I had asked a question borne out of my own ignorance. Being a newly minted Ph.D. with Edwin Gordon to my credit, I was curious to know whether Frauke Haasemann had a pedagogical order to her warm-ups. Had I been more astute and thoughtful, I probably would not have asked such a question. But I must confess, I was as guilty in those early days of not being pedagogically perceptive as many of my graduate students are today. In a telephone conversation, I asked her if she had an "order" to what she did? In all my years with this remarkable woman, I always knew her as a deeply caring and patient teacher—with the exception of this day! She replied to me very curtly, "Yes, there is an order. I will send it to you!"

In a few days, a single-page letter arrived at my home in Connecticut. The letter was typed on Frauke's manual typewriter. It said, simply: "Dear James, Here is The List." Note the capital letters! While I did not mean to imply that her pedagogy was scattershot, the fact that I did not perceive "The List" before she sent me "The List" is the same problem many of my students experience. One of the hallmarks of great pedagogy is that when tightly constructed, it may be difficult to analyze its component parts without some direction. For me, a rigid compliance to "The List" (a/k/a the Group Vocal Technique "method") must be basic to all warm-ups.

---

22 Some fifty hours of unedited footage are in the Talbot Library Archives at Westminster Choir College, which includes her entire summer session course!

Many conductors think it is okay to skip a step. My experience has taught me that if I miss a step (or even just re-shuffle the pedagogical order), the rehearsal that follows is never vocally "right." The strictest adherence to "The List" will reap incredible benefits toward the individual vocal health of your choir *and* the vocal sanity of the rehearsal that is to follow.

THE LIST

Required in Every Warm-Up:

- Relaxation
- Alignment
- Relaxation of the Vocal Tract – The Sigh
- Breathing – Inhalation/Exhalation – Eight-Handed Breathing
- "Support" as Applied to Sung Exercises
- Resonance
- General Resonance/Specific Resonance
- Vowel Development Hierarchy – "oo" and "ee" or German "ü"

Enrichment Preparing for the Rehearsal to Follow:

- Dynamics
- Crescendo/Decrescendo
- Range Extension Upward (every warm-up?)
- Range Extension Downward
- Leaps
- Legato
- Staccato
- Martellato
- Diction Teaching: Three-Step Procedure

WHAT IS ESSENTIAL?

Frauke Haasemann taught me that there are certain factors within "The List" that are important pedagogical markers, and the elements of "The List" must be followed in a strict pedagogical order. To depart from the order creates a sonic imbalance within the instrument. If taken into the choral rehearsal, tone that is not built in a pedagogically ordered fashion will create sonic havoc throughout the rehearsal that follows. One step in "The List" taken out of order will create a domino effect within the rehearsal that follows that is difficult to repair outside of the warm-up process.

Of all the steps in "The List," many conductors forget to perform the sigh—a rejuvenating sigh not only at the beginning of the warm-up process, but also interspaced between exercises. There is perhaps no more important step in readying the voice for rehearsal than the correct execution of the sigh. The function of the sigh is somewhat diagnostic. It gives conductors a clue as to whether the laryngeal position of the singers is advantageous for singing.

The sigh downward should only be performed on an "oo" or "ee" vowel or the German "ü." Male voices should not begin a downward sigh in falsetto because by doing so, they bypass their head tone register. The soft palate should be raised throughout, and the sound should be maintained high and forward as the sound descends. The vowels chosen for the sigh should be slightly closed.

In "The List" that appears on the previous page, the "required" steps and their sequence require the attention of every conductor in every warm-up. Aside from the sigh, the essential "tone building" part of every warm-up is the resonance part of the warm-up sequence.[23]

HARMONIC VS. MELODY ONLY EXERCISES

For techniques and pedagogies that support both vocal health and building listening abilities that result in in-tune singing, we must consider an overall adjustment in philosophy of both the choral warm-up and the rehearsal process. For years, conductors used unison vocalises as the primary vehicle for "warming up" a choir. More recent practices and considerable amounts of research point to inefficiencies and inherent hazards of warming up singers in unison. While one could argue that there is no immediate "damage" and that certain listening skills can be taught within a warm-up, the aural evidence now supported by research should tip our pedagogical scales toward harmonically based warm-ups.

As an instrumentalist, I learned to play in tune by listening to everyone but myself and to tune within a larger harmonic structure. In essence, I learned that it is only harmonic context that determines intonation. Melodic intonation is different than harmonic intonation![24]

---

23 Specific exercises for this are detailed in the books *Ear Training Immersion Exercises for Choirs and The Choral Warm-Up* (both texts are published by GIA).

24 One of the definitive works regarding choral intonation that distinguishes between melodic intonation and harmonic intonation is *Choral Intonation* by Gunnar Alldahl (Gehrmans Musikförlag, 1990).

THE "SECOND DEGREE" INTONATION TRAP

I have found that new educational ideas seem to have a life of their own. What begins as a concept, if accepted by teachers, soon demands appropriate materials. Additionally, as we teach, clarity of thought and additional ideas and concepts are presented from our work with the materials. But most exciting is the process an author goes through. The metamorphosis of an idea is a blessing. One step seems to logically lead to another and another. All of this grows out of a desire to improve the music teaching/learning process.

An example is *Choral Ensemble Intonation* (published in 2001), which presents an approach to choral ensemble solfège called "Harmonic Immersion Solfege." This approach grew out of my background as an instrumentalist. Instrumentalists acquire music literacy skills via ensemble experiences. It occurred to me that for years, choral ensembles have worked in a way that was almost the polar opposite to how instrumental ensembles learn music. In fact, choral ensembles are in "learning opposition" to many other types of instrumental ensembles.

In language, most of what we learn about our language is learned and derived through syntax. This idea is fundamental to all of the ideas presented by Edwin Gordon in defining a Music Learning Theory, as detailed in *Learning Sequences in Music*.[25] New word meaning in language is derived from the "meaning" of already known words that surround it. Generally, words are not learned independently, apart from their syntax. In fact, it has been shown that words or phrases that are not used and acquired within a harmonic context are not retained. I am convinced that musicians learn music the same way language is acquired. I also believe that we are not capitalizing on the potent power of the choral ensemble to provide the aural syntax for learning. Using Harmonic Immersion Solfege, a melody or a single line is never performed without its harmonic syntactical surroundings. While it may seem to be a stupendously simple concept, my experience the past five years has proven to me, beyond doubt, that this prescribed method is deeply rich with pedagogical benefits for both vocalism and intonation.

It has become apparent to me that as a part of the ensemble warm-up, we need materials that provide a rich harmonic syntax for singers to hear. Further,

---

25 Edwin E. Gordon, *Learning Sequences in Music, 2012 Edition* (Chicago: GIA Publications, 1998, 2003, 2007, 2012).

beyond major mode, there is a pressing need for these materials to be available in all modes. It should not be underestimated the amount of music learning that can take place by constant immersion in these sounds. The power of musical syntax establishes in the musical mind the relationships and functions of harmonies within each mode—all without the knowledge of written music theory. In the nineteenth century, Lowell Mason believed the ear must be developed before the eye. Somehow, in the intervening time, musicians have diverged from this basic teaching principle.

Some musicians I know have contempt for this process. They are also musicians who have perfect pitch and have never had a need for such "musical assistance" or "ear training." Unfortunately, however, the majority of those who sing in our church, school, and college choirs do not have an understanding of the aural language of music. Many persons say they are not musicians. The problem is they have been bombarded with systems of music teaching that do not focus upon strengthening the ear before the eye. And the solution is that the choral warm-up is the perfect opportunity to strengthen the ear devoid of notation while building in habits of good singing.

CHAPTER 11
AUDIATION AND IMAGING
THE KEY— "PRACTICING" CONDUCTING[26]

James Jordan

Don't fly your plane anywhere where your mind has not been first.

> —John McDonald,
> a flight instructor in a private flying lesson

Man moves in order to satisfy a need. He aims his movement at something of value to him. It is easy to perceive the aim of a person's movement if it is directed at some tangible object. Yet there also exist intangible values that inspire movement. (p. 129)

> —Rudolf von Laban in *Beyond Words*,
> Carol-Lynne Moore and Kaoru Yamamoto

Following one another in movement sequences, the consecutive efforts will build up a kind of melody or sentence-like structure, the collective mood of which is an important part of movement experience. (p. 46)

> —Rudolf Laban in
> *Modern Educational Dance*

---

26 The author of this book would like to thank Eugene Migliaro Corporon for sharing his insight on these principles.

Kinesthesis (the "muscle sense" or "sixth sense") is defined as the sensual discrimination of the positions and movement of body parts based on information other than visual, auditory, or verbal. Kinesthetic perception involves judging changes in muscle tension, body position, and the relative placement of body parts. (p. 48)

Human body movement is an ever-present, complex, and yet an elusive part of our lives, subject to "tune out," simplification, and other perceptual maneuvers. The first task facing the movement observer is to find ways to enhance awareness and to sharpen and crystallize motion perception. (p. 65)
Since body movement leaves no artifacts or traces behind, reconstructing this leap requires some imagination. (p. 74)

In a sense, movement awareness is often the victim of tune-out. As you recall, our perceptual systems are designed to cease to register a stimulus that is repeated again and again. (p. 85)

Yet another view is manifested in the metaphor, "Movement is a private code." Here, movement is seen to have neither panhuman nor even culture-specific meanings, but only unique and individualistic senses to it. That is, each person uses body movement somewhat idiosyncratically, thus conveying meanings that are unique to him or her. (p. 114)

—Carol-Lynne Moore and
Kaoru Yamamoto in *Beyond Words*

One must learn to understand that one thinks not only with the brain but also with the little finger and the big toe. (p. 67)

—Rudolf Steiner in *Beyond Words*,
Carol-Lynne Moore and Kaoru Yamamoto

Sound itself is not music. Sound becomes music through audiation, when, as with language, you translate sounds in your mind and give them meaning. The meaning you give to these sounds will be different depending on the occasion and will be different from the meaning given them by any other person. Audiation is the process of assimilating and comprehending (not simply rehearing) music we have just heard performed or have heard performed sometime in the past. (pp. 3–4)

Imitation is learning through someone else's ears. Audiation is learning through one's own ears. Imitation is analogous to using tracing paper to draw a picture, whereas audiation is analogous to visualizing and then drawing a picture. Imitation is like painting a canvas; it deals with both the essential and nonessential. Audiation is like sculpture; it emphasizes the essential. Just as you must think for yourself, so must you audiate for yourself. You imitate when you repeat what you heard just a few seconds ago, which is immediate imitation, or when you repeat what you heard a while ago, which is delayed imitation. In either case, they are reactive responses and have only initial and limited value for learning, because unless we audiate what we have just imitated, we soon forget it, as is so often the case, for example, with the names and dates children learn in school. However, audiation is a different kind of learning because when you audiate, you retain, instantiate, and "think about" what you heard seconds, minutes, hours, days, weeks, months, or even years ago. Audiation is an active response. When we imitate we know what to perform next in familiar music by remembering what we just performed. It is a process of looking backward. However, when we audiate we know what to perform next, without negating memory, by anticipating in familiar music and predicting in unfamiliar music what is to come. It involves forward thinking. What is audiated plays a formidable role in how one learns. What we audiate is never forgotten. It becomes a component of more complex audiation. In cognitive terms, the structure of audiation is deep and serves in background conception. The structure of imitation, on the other hand, is superficial and serves simply as foreground perception. (p. 10)

—Edwin E Gordon in
Learning Sequences in Music (2007 Edition)

Mr. Fleischer describes the performer as three people in one. "Person A hears before they play. They have to have this ideal in their inner ear of what they're going to try and realize. Person B actually puts the keys down, plays and tries to manifest what person A hears. Person C sits a little bit apart and listens. And if what C hears is not what A intended, C tells B to adjust to get closer to what A wanted. And this goes on with every note you play, no matter how fast you're playing. It's a simultaneous process that advances horizontally. When it works, when it all meshes, it's a state of ecstasy." (p. 27)

Life knocks the corners off; age, or experience, accounts for some degree of transformation in every artist. One hears new implications. I think one has a tendency to take more time. One listens and takes more time to listen. One is not afraid to more deeply characterize certain ideas. Silence is not the absence of music. Play, judiciously, as late as possible, without being late. (p. 25)

Mr. Fleisher is convinced that he is a better pianist for having become a conductor, as he would probably not have done had his career stayed on course. He may also be, he says, a better teacher...with his remarkable ability to articulate musical ideas in images. He describes a tune as "rising the way a balloon does, at an ever-decreasing rate of speed, to the point where the pressure out- side equals the pressure inside, and it stays suspended." He talks about conducting an orchestra around a curve in the musical line and generating the sort of centrifugal force that causes the driver of a car to lean to the left as he turns his wheels to the right. (p. 27)

—Leon Fleischer in "A Pianist for Whom Never
Was Never an Option" Holly Brubach
The New York Times, Sunday, June 10, 2007

I believe that it is accurate to say that most Alexander teachers regard the Technique as one bright strand in the large braid of somatics, but some do not. Some want to claim a status for the Technique as unique, outside somatics, and rightly understood only in contrast to other disciplines. In this argument the teachers look not to the results (they acknowledge that many techniques result in greater freedom and ease of movement and the recovery of body awareness) but to the means. No other method features constructive conscious control, the cognitive process that Alexander used to recover his freedom.

Constructive conscious control exploits the brain's vast potential for consciousness of self and for choice. Some prominent neuroscientists believe that self-consciousness (in the good sense) and choice depend on the size and structure of the human brain. Both the size and structure make it possible for the brain to process its own functioning (creatures with smaller, differently structured brains cannot do this), resulting in consciousness. Alexander's Technique uses the brain consciously for self-observation of habitual use of the organism, for conscious inhibition of habitual use, for conscious observation of an emerging, more integrated use, for conscious cooperation with the more integrated use, and even for conscious observation of the more integrated use, all this depending surely on the conscious linking of conceptual and motor functions in the brain, by choice. Rather than creating a split, as some might expect, all this consciousness instead has a profoundly integrating effect, healing the split many people experience between thinking and being, of mind and body, or consciousness and functioning. It is this integration that is the great good the Technique offers, with freedom and ease as by-products, according to this argument.

—Barbara Conable from article on
www.AlexanderTechnique.com

The term somatics was first introduced into modern psychology by Thomas Hanna with his book Bodies in Revolt. The Greek word soma is defined as "the body experienced from within" and reflects the efforts of modern bodywork practitioners and somatic move- ment therapists to move away from the dualistic splitting of mind from body, towards a model of integrated functioning of the whole person, psyche and soma. (p. 11)

—Linda Hartley in *Somatic Psychology*

The term *audiation*, coined by Edwin Gordon to describe the process by which we hear and recall music, has become part of the vocabulary for all who believe that the teaching of listening is fundamental to music learning. Briefly stated, the broad definition of audiation is the ability to hear sound in all its dimensions without the sound being physically present. Dr. Gordon details both the types and stages of audiation in two of his books, *Preparatory Audiation, Audiation, and Music Learning Theory* (GIA,

2001) and *Learning Sequences in Music* (GIA, 2007). To thoroughly understand the audiation process, which is part of becoming an aware conductor, it is helpful to be familiar with the types and stages of audiation so you can appreciate the many dimensions of hearing. To simply call this complex process "inner hearing" can cause us to hear in a very shallow or incomplete manner. Becoming aurally facile with the depth of the audiation process is part of "becoming aware."

As a conductor, no one would likely argue that "hearing" a score is the product of careful score preparation. But the question I find interesting is: How do we as conductors transfer what we hear, or rather have learned to hear through score study and subsequent audiation, to gestures that communicate our intent to an ensemble? I believe that process occurs when we *simultaneously* audiate and image our conducting as part of our regular practice routine.

Consider this: Athletes in certain sports rely on imaging to practice. For example, because it may not be convenient to do repeated ski runs, skiers might practice mentally, imagining their movement (i.e., practicing through a sort of movement audiation). As another example, dancers imagine themselves moving when they are not practicing. The science of somatics has informed our knowledge of how the brain maps, in a cognitive way, the motion of our body and how we move. The skill we must develop as conductors is to merge sound audiation with what I call *kinesthetic imaging*. We must be able to move while audiating and listening. To imagine our conducting movement separate from audiation will not help us master this important skill.

In psychology, the perception of movement (more particularly, the self-perception of movement) has not been experimentally studied because it is difficult to come up with a research design that provides objective data. While there have been many hypotheses on how we perceive our own motion while moving, studies have not yielded valid objective data.

There is an important principle to understand about conducting. The process of conducting, in essence, occurs before sound actually takes place in the ensemble. Ensemble sound ideally occurs slightly after the sound is birthed through breath and gestural impulse on the part of the conductor. The process becomes more complex when we react to the sound we are is hearing—which is, in essence, after the sound was created, or in its past! If we do not practice audiating and imaging simultaneously, then in rehearsal we are merely reacting to sound "in the moment." Conducting that is not informed by audiation/imaging is essentially conducting without the creative or germinal musical impulse present! The result is a series of reactions that lack the creative initiation of sound that can only be birthed by an impulse before each sound is created. Instead, we should consider the initial marriage of gesture and sound to be born out of multi-dimensional forethought rather than afterthought. Consider a visual paradigm of this process *(see Figure 11-1)*.

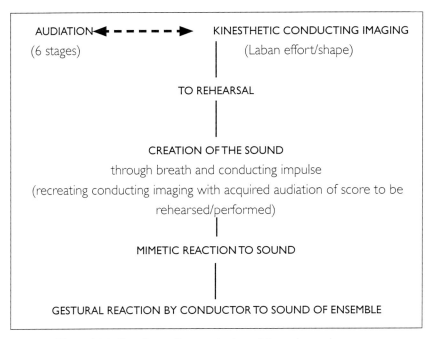

Figure 11.1. Paradigm of score study and the rehearsal process.

KINESTHETIC AUDIATION: MOVEMENT IMAGING

We can imagine ourselves moving; however, this is probably one of our least used perceptual gifts. By understanding the use of Laban effort/shape, we awaken our perceptions (or awarenesses) regarding how we move, and we have a vehicle by which we can recall what it feels like to move without actually moving in space! Just as the audiation of music can be developed, the imaging of one's movement must also be learned and practiced.

The marriage of sound to movement is a unique process for conductors that must be an integral part of the score preparation process. We cannot assume that by "knowing the score" we will automatically and intuitively make the connection between how the work "moves" and how we would move with the sound present. The perception of one's moving self is powerful. Audiation is powerful. But they must be bound to each other in some way that makes them a symbiotic, interdependent whole before we enter rehearsal!

MIMETIC INTUITIVE RESPONSE TO SOUND

Another factor that could sabotage a conductor's careful thought and study of a score is the theory of mimetics, or in other words, the "envy of the perfect sound" that is omnipresent in our own personal musical world.[27] If we do not stay in "the right place" when things go wrong in rehearsal, most often the first thing to change is our gesture, which carries both our conscious and subconscious musical intent. Instead, if we continue to "image" the movement we envisioned in our score study process, then we can ensure a correct mimetical environment in which the choir can musically grow and listen. In other words, we must stay in awareness as a conductor.

Listening, audiating, and imaging must occur concurrently for musicing to be transformed through our conducting to a level that transcends our music from mundane group parody to the creation of a personal experience with a work of art. We must believe it to be so. That is, we must trust that our ensemble will follow us on our journey so our audiation and imaging can continue to lead the way in our rehearsal process.

A SYMBIOTIC PROCESS

Score preparation must contain equal parts of score study and kinesthetic imaging. The process of imagining how you will move after you have studied the score and have an audiational sense of the score will move your score study and your rehearsals to new levels. Conducting, then, becomes an active recreation of what you have studied in sound and imagined in movement. Simply studying the score will not ensure you can move to the score with gesture that is musically meaningful. While reaction to sound in rehearsal is certainly spontaneous, the basic boundaries of how we move as conductors cannot be. Our self-perception of movement must precede the act of moving in union with music by imaging our movement while concurrently audiating the score in all its dimensions. We

---

25 For more on mimetics, the reader is referred to *The Musician's Soul* (GIA, 1999) and *The Musician's Walk* (GIA, 2006) by this author.

can indeed practice conducting prior to rehearsal by audiating the score and imagining how we will conduct the score.[28] Do not underestimate the power of this type of somatic preparation and its effectiveness as part of the score preparation process.

> Approaching the unconscious through attending to the body,
> we gain access to a great range and depth of sensory and emotional experience.
> We begin by listening inwardly to the flow of sensations, images, feelings, sounds,
> memories, and movement impulses which emerge into awareness. (p. 62)
>
> —Linda Hartley in *Somatic Psychology*

> One may be said to "own" or "possess" one's body—at least its limbs and
> movable parts—by virtue of a constant flow of incoming information, arising
> ceaselessly, throughout life, from the muscles, joints, and tendons. One has oneself,
> one is oneself, because the body knows itself, confirms itself, at all times, by this
> sixth sense. (p. 47)
>
> —Oliver Sacks in *Beyond Words*,
> Carol-Lynne Moore ru Yamamoto

---

26 As part of this "visualization" process, it is important for conductors to correctly imagine how the bodymoves as one conducts. For more in-depth study, reference the DVD, *The Anatomy of Conducting*, by James Jordan and Eugene Migliaro Corporon (GIA, 2007).

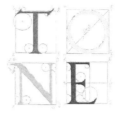

CHAPTER 12

SUPPORTING SINGING AND LISTENING THROUGH CHORAL ACCOMPANYING

Jonathan Palmer Lakeland

A NOTE IN DEFENSE OF THE CHORAL ACCOMPANIST

Until Gerald Moore rose to prominence on the concert scene, the art of song accompanying was plodding steadily towards an unwarranted demise. This great genre of classical music was doomed to a life of servitude in the serfdom of the singer. Such enslavement not only restrained the pianist but also, consequently, restrained the message, meaning, and potential human connection of the music.

Gerald Moore, through his superb teaching and accompanying witty commentary, opened the eyes of musicians and music lovers alike. He introduced a new understanding of the importance of song accompanying and the colorful palette of tools that song accompanists have at their disposal. Before Gerald Moore, there were many musicians and music lovers who never would have dreamed of thinking of the art of accompanying in such vivid detail. When we absorb and distill all of the knowledge he shared, we arrive at the understanding that song accompanists are equal partners in the music-making experience. They have the same responsibilities, the same influence, and they must approach their music making with the same care as the singers.

FROM SIDESHOW TO (CO)-RING LEADER

Choral accompanists are often fiercely supported by the choirs and conductors with whom they work. These collaborators value the time and effort that choral accompanists spend in rehearsal and performance. They value their musical input and pianistic skill. If you ask collaborators, however, what their accompanists do beyond providing a background track to choral singing, many will respond with blank, confused faces.

Very often, the choral accompanist is a sideshow—plodding away on an accompanying part written by the composer or waiting in elegant silence for the next time they get to ring out a series of pitches. Many conductors, even many great conductors, comfortably say that accompanists have no responsibilities beyond their traditional role. These outright "No's" are understandable; they are a reflection of centuries upon centuries of musical tradition where choirs rehearsed without the aid of any keyboard instruments at all.

There is no arguing that some choirs have sung exceedingly well without the aid of keyboard instruments for a long time. In the last 100 years, however, there have been great advances made to musical composition and to the arts of choral conducting and singing. Choral accompanists still live in a very pre-Gerald Moore world, where the influence and responsibility of the choral accompanist in the modern choral rehearsal is greatly misunderstood.

During my time as the principal accompanist for James Jordan and the Westminster Williamson Voices, built upon the work of my predecessor Marilyn Shenenberger, we came to a realization that there is now a need to update the required skill set and job description of the choral accompanist. In the past 100 years, the developments made in choral conducting and in choral music composition require a new kind of choral accompanist—a musical colleague, not a musical servant.

Not surprisingly, it all begins with the breath.

SUPPORTING BREATH AND THE FIRST SOUND

If we, the choral accompanists, are to directly complement the conductor's gesture with sound, we must begin to think not just in musical terms, but in pedagogical terms as well. We must not simply be focused on the product, but also on the journey that determines the product. Pedagogy is that journey. Good pedagogy is built upon an understanding of the student's, or group of students', inherent strengths and weaknesses, the understood and the misunderstood, that which exists and that which is yet to come.

We could write volumes and volumes over the potential minefield that is rehearsal and performance. Perhaps the most vulnerable moment in both the rehearsal and performance processes is the moment just as the music is beginning: from before the first breath until after the first sound.

I did not fully realize how vulnerable this moment is until I began to spend time accompanying for James Jordan's conducting lessons. We would spend a great amount of time with students exploring the depth of this topic. It is very easy for a conductor to provide unnecessary or unhelpful information at this vulnerable moment. Such misinformation can cause any number of major problems, including breath, pitch, intonation, and a breakdown in ensemble communication, to name a few.

Let us not forget, however, that in much choral music, the first piece of information the choir receives comes not from the conductor, but from the accompanist! How can we believe that the conductor must take such necessary care and dedication in showing a breath impulse gesture, but also believe that the opening pitches require none of that same care and dedication? Inconceivable!

The obvious conclusion is that accompanists need to have a corresponding breath impulse gesture to complement and match the conductor's breath impulse gesture. It must help support and solidify the ensemble in the same ways as the conductor's, but instead of being visual, it must be aural. Is that best accomplished by the accompanist mechanically plodding some pitches onto the piano, or instead by taking a careful and analytic approach?

I HAVE 99 PROBLEMS, AND A PITCH IS CERTAINLY ONE OF THEM

At this moment, my mind's eye is broadcasting the image of a successful choral accompanist who is sitting in his house reading this book. He sips his tea and intently questions every word that is written here (as I hope all of you do). He looks at these sentences skeptically, quite sure that every word written here is complete rubbish. His inner monologue says, "What's to think about? We are just playing the pitches! We play them, and get them out of the way. It's simple. Don't overcomplicate it."

Well, my dear skeptical readers, I understand your reservations. I would not postulate that a brainless plodding of the opening pitches would cause a complete, unfixable train wreck. Choirs are complex musical machines, with a great amount of resilience. Instead, I would postulate that brainless plodding of the opening pitches is what keeps a *good* choir from becoming a *great* choir.

Supporting the choir in this vulnerable state is tricky. We have to first analyze the opening of the piece by defining its musical characteristics in the following ways:

- What voice part(s) enter first?
- Does the piece begin with a true unison, unison with octave displacement, or harmonic?
- What are the opening dynamics/mood of the moment?
- What is the opening texture and soundscape of the work?

WHICH VOICE PART(S) ENTER FIRST?

When we provide pitches for the opening of a piece, we are providing a vast array of musical information to the choir. The ensemble will (subconsciously or consciously) convert all of this information to their voices. We must be sure that all of the musical information we provide is relevant and accurate to the music that is about to be sung. This begins with choosing the appropriate register in which to provide the pitches.

Much like opera repetiteurs, who have to emulate the sound of an orchestra at all times, we choral accompanists need to begin emulating the sound of the choir when we give pitches. Providing musical information in registers that naturally sound very pianistic will only distract the ears of the singers. Instead, we should play pitches in octaves on the piano that sound pure. To accomplish this, pitches should generally be provided in the third or fourth octaves of the piano (the octave below and above middle C). These octaves are usually the clearest octaves on the piano, and they best emulate the sound of a voice.

Gratefully, there is much choral repertoire that already begins in this range. Some pieces begin outside of these two octaves, and we will be tempted to give pitches in the octave that is written. This is only logical. It will better serve the singers, however, if we provide pitches in the third and fourth octaves, asking the singers to audiate their pitch in the correct octave. Aside from an overly pianistic sound being distracting, I have previously experienced a number of occasions when singers were frightened when they heard the pitch on which they were to enter. All in all, I have found it to be a safe and good practice to provide pitches, as much as possible, in the third and fourth octaves of the piano.

You may find that ensembles with untrained or less-experienced singers struggle with this approach. As a rule of thumb, we should always give the singers what they need, but actively help them to develop new and existing skills as much as possible.

Does the piece begin with a true unison, unison with octave displacement, or harmonic?

- **True unison** – In a true unison opening, where all voices begin on exactly the same pitch in the same octave, play that pitch.

- **Unison with octave displacement** – In this example, where all voices begin on the same pitch in different octaves, play the highest pitch that is sung within the third or fourth octaves.

- **Harmonic** – When we encounter a piece that begins with harmony, we are faced with an interesting challenge. Choirs and pianos are tuned very differently. Choirs can tune to the harmonic structure. Pianos cannot adjust the intonation of individual pitches to match the harmonic structure. Consequently, a third (for example) as it is heard on the piano does not match how a choir will sing a third. In lieu of this, we want to provide the pitches in a way that gives accurate pitch information but does not force the choir to adjust its tuning to the piano. To do this, I very carefully plan which pitches I will play.

Harmony as Written	What We Play (Solfège)
Diad of a fifth	"Do"
Diad of a second, fourth, sixth, or seventh	Play as written
Diad of third	Play "Do" (or lower note of the third)
Triad in root position	"Do" – "Sol"
Triad in first inversion	"Do" – "So" – "Do"[(8va)]
Triad in second inversion	"So" – "Do" – "So"[(8va)]
Non-diatonic or highly chromatic harmonies	Even the most advanced ensembles may need each individual pitch given. Provide the pitches as written, but attempt to wean the choir off of this as soon as possible.

WHAT ARE THE OPENING DYNAMICS/ MOOD OF THE MOMENT?

The accompanist must continue to remember that the pitches are the first piece of musical information the choir receives. They are an audible equivalent to the breath impulse gesture. The breath impulse gesture is, above all, an invitation: it invites the choir to sing, to sing with unified meaning and intention, and to sing as an ensemble. The accompanist's breath impulse gesture must be the same kind of invitation.

When conductors learn about showing the breath impulse gesture, they are taught how to consider every aspect of the music. Dynamics and mood of the music are a part of the musical details that must be considered.

Let's say you are approached by a new acquaintance. This "Energetic Eddie" races towards you saying, "Hi! Nice to meet you!" in a bright, cheery, and loud expression. Your first encounter with Eddie makes you feel a certain way about him and evokes from you a particular mood and tone in your response.

Next, you are approached by another new acquaintance: "Shy Sam." Sam slinks towards you and utters a sheepish, "Hello. How are you?" in a hushed and quiet tone. You certainly would not respond like you did to Eddie. Quite the contrary: you would instinctually respond in a mood and tone similar to Sam's.

The choir reacts the same way when singers hear a piece of musical information. The accompanist is imparting not only pitch content, but also a reminder of the tone, mood, and intention of the piece. Thus, the breath impulse gesture is an invitation. This requires the accompanist to be sure the pitches given fit within the musical and dynamic world of the piece.

WHAT IS THE OPENING TEXTURE AND SOUNDSCAPE OF THE WORK?

After analyzing the previous musical elements of the opening, the accompanist can play the opening pitches and find that the choir still struggles with the opening. Context is the final piece of musical information we need to provide as accompanist.

When examining the texture and soundscape of the opening, we are analyzing how the composer has constructed the music. Understanding this musical architecture is imperative for both the conductor and accompanist. In moments when the composer writes a challenging opening, we may need to provide some additional musical context to the choir.

There are many instances that can be found between this practice in music and similar practices in other art forms. Actors may need to call for a "line" in rehearsal. A public speaker may need to refer to his or her notes. An opera singer may need help from a prompter. It is important that when a performing artist is in trouble, he or she gets the assistance needed. In a choral rehearsal, it may be necessary (particularly as a choir is learning a piece) to have the singers' minds and ears refreshed as to the nature of the music.

At this point, many readers might think this will cause the accompanist to become a crutch, as opposed to a pedagogue. It is true that the line between these two states of being can be thin. Therefore, I use the following definitions of the two terms to examine my actions at the keyboard:

As accompanists, we are *pedagogues* if we use a technique to transmit or communicate musical information, and then transfer the responsibility for the recall and application of this information to the choir. We accomplish this by steadily reducing the use of the technique, which consequently requires the choir to take ownership of the knowledge. We should continue to reduce the use of the technique until we are providing only the most pertinent and essential musical information that ensures the quality of the choir's performance will not be sacrificed.

As accompanists, we are being a "crutch" if we use a technique to communicate musical information but not transfer responsibility of this knowledge. The more a choir gets used to hearing the accompanist provide the information, the more they will rely on this information, to their own detriment.

By this logic, we are still being pedagogues if we provide the choir with more than just the opening pitches, as long as the additional information is necessary. This means that in some instances, we may provide a fragment of the opening melody. In other instances, we may provide a few of the first chords. In still other instances, the choir may be able to find the opening pitch of a new piece from the final pitch of the previous piece. Whatever the situation, we must make sure we are pedagogues and not crutches.

THE LAKE ISLE OF INNISFREE

William Butler Yeats (1865–1939)   Thomas LaVoy

Figure 12.1. Lavoy, *The Lake Isle of Innisfree.*

Having worked a number of times on this excellent piece (*see Figure 12.1*), *The Lake Isle of Innisfree* by my friend Thomas LaVoy, I know that the choir often needs to hear some of the musical context. This is mainly due to the stunning, yet tricky bass entrance. So in rehearsal, I would provide:

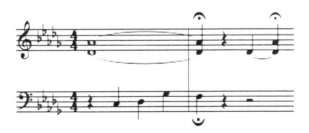

Figure 12.2. Providing musical context.

The choir hears:

- The soprano and alto opening pitches;
- The bass line;
- A break in the sound to clear the air; and
- The soprano and alto opening pitches (now broken and sustained).

The silence and re-sounding of the two opening pitches is essential. The silence wipes the slate clean. It is as if the choir has glanced at a sunset and now stares at the blank canvas, preparing to paint. Re-sounding the two opening pitches sets the harmonic context for the sopranos and altos, which the basses will use this to inform their opening pitches. It is the painter remembering the sunset as he or she brings brush to palette, and palette to canvas.

THE PITCH RITUAL

Up to this point, we have examined a new approach to giving pitches. It took years for me to even notice that there was a better way to do this seemingly mindless task. As soon as I realized that the choir made far fewer mistakes when I provided the pitches as I detailed above, it was clear that this was not just superfluous hypothesizing.

My new approach systemizes how the accompanist provides pitches relative to the compositional structure of a piece of music. Through this systemization comes a pattern—the *pitch ritual*. The goal is to provide all of the necessary musical information, with no needless or harmful musical information. With the choir able to place more trust in the accompanist, as well as the strengthened relationship between conductor and accompanist, singers are able to feel comforted and supported in their moment of greatest vulnerability. This altered state of mind means that the pitch ritual creates a somewhat "Pavlovian" response within the singers, which acts as an autonomous shortcut for the singers to easily find a more focused, prepared, and centered self.

The pitch ritual is an important and helpful tool. It depends first on deep attention to musical detail, as we have already examined. Second, it depends on repetition: that as often as possible the accompanist is using this approach, thereby subconsciously instilling a sense of order within the choir. The third, and as of yet undiscussed, aspect of the pitch ritual is that it must rhythmically complement the conductor's breath impulse gesture.

Returning to the previous example of LaVoy's *The Lake Isle of Innisfree*, how do we rhythmically complement the breath impulse gesture (*see Figure 12.3*)?

Figure 12.3. Breath impulse gesture.

First, we must remember that the creation of silence is a musical event, just like the creation of the first sound. All musical events have rhythm. So to rhythmically complement the breath impulse gesture, we must release our opening pitches on the ictus of the breath impulse gesture. By sounding a musical event on the breath impulse gesture, we emphasize that first beat. This highlights, and consequently unifies, the tempo and the pulse of the piece.

THE COMPLEMENTARY ACCOMPANIST

So far, we have examined one specific way in which the accompanist can work as a complement to the conductor. Of course, it goes without saying that for the accompanist to work as a complement to the conductor, the conductor must also work as a complement to the accompanist. This collaboration is the cornerstone of the modern choral rehearsal and performance.

To be a true complement to the conductor, we must constantly ask ourselves: How can I take the musical and pedagogical intention of the conductor's gesture and translate it into sound that can be created at the piano? To answer this question, we must have a rich understanding all of the concepts and skills the conductor must master.

Young choral conductors spend great amounts of time learning how to plan a rehearsal and use rehearsal techniques to draw the best possible musical performance out of an ensemble. Having spent a vast amount of time with James

Jordan in both the rehearsal room and the classroom, I have been able to see this truth firsthand. What James Jordan and I both have come to understand through our time in both the rehearsal room and the classroom is that when the choir is learning and polishing a new piece, the accompanist has a clear and distinct pedagogical role.

The following is based upon knowledge I gained both from James Jordan and from my piano teacher at Westminster, Dr. James Goldsworthy. Without this knowledge working in tandem, I would never have been able to experiment with these ideas and stumble across a new, exciting, and enriching way for the accompanist to be an essential part of the choral rehearsal.

FROM COMPREHENSION TO CONCERT

Dr. James Goldsworthy, my piano teacher during my time as an undergraduate at Westminster Choir College, is one of the great piano pedagogues alive today. His genius is widely recounted by his current and previous students, and his warm, welcoming, intellectual, and wildly engaging personality is known by all of the Westminster community. He has shaped my musical world and turned me into a better musician than I have any right to be. He set me on the path to a lifelong love of learning and an infectious desire to communicate, from the deepest part of my being, what I find to be the true intention of the composer.

One of the many things he teaches his students is that rhythm is the underdog in the family of musical elements. Melody and harmony often get to be celebrities, while rhythm takes a back seat. We are all guilty of neglecting rhythm at one time or another. There is something within us that is drawn to melody and harmony, but we tend to overlook the importance and the influence of rhythm.

My early lessons with Dr. Goldsworthy were filled with realizations of the following truth:

Rhythm → Harmony → Melody

or more specifically

Rhythm (influences) Harmony (which influences) Melody

Melody cannot exist without rhythm and, at the very least, an implication of harmony. Harmony can exist without melody, but cannot exist without rhythm.

Rhythm *can* exist without melody and harmony. Because we are prone to overlooking it, beginning with learning the rhythm of a piece (including note durations, meter, and harmonic rhythm) is essential to fully learning a piece of music. This is a cornerstone for how James Jordan and I work with the Westminster Williamson Voices as conductor and accompanist.

INTRODUCING A NEW PIECE

THE FIRST READING

When the Williamson singers pick up a new piece for the first time, we begin with a first reading. Unless the piece is very well known to the choir, this first reading is unsung. The choir is told to sit and listen to the accompanist play through the piece.

For me at this point, playing every pitch of every vocal line is not the most important goal. The top priority is to provide an accurate recreation of the rhythm and harmony of the piece. Technical capability paired with this priority may prevent it from being possible to play every note, and that's okay. We must provide the choir with, at the very least, a sense of the pulse, meter, harmonic rhythm, and harmonic progression of the piece.

Usually, the choir is told to follow along in their scores while I play the piece. They are not instructed to audiate the vocal lines, but instead are told to listen to the harmonic rhythm and progression of the piece. The harmonic rhythm and progression teach us so much about the music. By studying this, the choir becomes deeply and instinctually aware of the form of the piece, the pulse, the harmony, other compositional techniques, and how every musical idea informs every other musical idea. This is experiential learning in its raw, purest form.

THE SECOND READING

The second reading is rather similar to the first. The accompanist again plays the piece through while the choir stays silent. This time, however, the singers are told to audiate their part. Now that the singers are aware of the harmonic progression and rhythm, they can begin to observe how their line fits into the equation, and the true meaning and reason for each note they sing. The singers should continue to listen intently to the harmonic rhythm and progression.

THE THIRD READING

Finally, the ever-patient choir gets to open their mouths and sing! After studying the score once, and then studying the score while audiating the vocal lines, the choir has a musical knowledge to stand on. If the choir has been aware of the musical information being provided, and I have done my job properly, the choir will have far fewer musical issues than they have ever had before. The reading will not be perfect, but because the choir now has an awareness of the piece, it will be a more informed sing-through than a cold read.

SIDENOTE: WHAT'S THE ACCOMPANIST'S JOB IN ALL OF THIS?

The accompanist plays a very influential role in these first readings. Often, the first readings are unconducted except in moments where the conductor wants something very specific and audible to happen in the music (e.g., tempo shift, etc.). As accompanists, we must be very careful in our first readings and be aware of a few important things that should be communicated.

As I mentioned previously, the most important goal is not to play every note, but instead to provide a highly accurate representation of the piece, paying particular attention to pulse, meter, rhythm, harmony (progression and rhythm), and melodic contours. We must also be sure to play the piece in a way that emulates the sound of the choir. This is a moment where I, for obvious reasons, tend to break one of the rules that I laid out in the section on giving pitches. In this case, emulating a choir has more to do with emulating *how* the choir will perform the piece, as opposed to making a tone that sounds like a choir.

Because a choir is far more resonant than a piano, I often double low octaves to achieve a fuller, richer bass sound. This also helps to highlight the bass line and its influence on the harmonic rhythm and progression. Much like in playing orchestral reductions, we also have to exercise the skill of knowing when to *not* embellish—and instead leave things out. If two vocal lines double each other, we can choose to play only one of them, giving our attention instead to the other aspects of the piece that need to be communicated. Attentiveness to where a choir will or will not breathe is also essential, as unified breaths in choirs (be it sectional or the full ensemble) are equivalent to serious rhythmic events. These are only some examples of information we must try to communicate.

If we represent the piece too pianistically, the choir will stop listening constructively and instead listen to the piece as if it was a piano piece. This is not what we should crave as accompanists. Instead, we must create a highly detailed and "musical" performance that reflects how the choir would sing the piece.

BEYOND THE READINGS

The third reading sets the choir on a musical journey. Following this reading, the accompanist and the conductor should use the following techniques to hone the choir's knowledge of the music and polish the choir's ability to perform the music. Before examining these techniques, we should keep the following ideas in mind:

- **Put yourself out of a job** – With a cappella choral repertoire, remove yourself from playing choral parts or using accompanied rehearsal techniques (*see below*) as soon as possible. We can be of immense help in the rehearsal of a cappella vocal music, but as soon as the singers have gained enough knowledge to stand on their own two feet, we must let them. We are always part of the ensemble, but at some point the choir must begin to take the responsibility of performing the piece.

- **Prepare for the unexpected** – No two choral rehearsals are ever the same. Conductors change their minds about rehearsal technique and musical decisions rather frequently. The accompanist has to be ready to switch to something new at any moment. Always be listening, aware, and reacting.

- **No singer(s) left behind**: One of the rules that James Jordan and I believe in the most is that no single voice part should be asked to sing alone. If a single voice part needs to be rehearsed, then some semblance of the harmony must also be provided. This is achieved by either asking two sections to sing together or by the accompanist jumping in to help. When singers are asked to sing without tuning to the harmonic progression, the singers will re-learn their intonation as if their line is the melody (which is not the case three-quarters of the time).

ACCOMPANIED REHEARSAL TECHNIQUES

There are a handful of accompanied or partly accompanied techniques that James Jordan and I use to teach music. These techniques can also work independently from, or in collaboration with, other rehearsal techniques.

Application of all of these techniques comes after the first three readings of the piece, when the choir is polishing and rehearsing specific moments of the piece.

Because of our extensive work together, rarely do we discuss implementing these techniques. Instead, these techniques sound as a gentle reminder from the keyboard to correct a certain problem or polish a certain moment. They require an ounce of subtlety from the accompanist and an ounce of acceptance and trust from the conductor that they will work.

So, below are a number of techniques that I have found myself implementing on a regular basis with the Westminster Williamson Voices. Together, these ideas form a regular rehearsal strategy that can work hand in hand with the approach of the conductor.

HARMONIC ENTRAINMENT

Harmony is quite possibly one of the musical elements we can effect the most. Because each singer tunes his or her pitches not to one preset pitch, but instead in relationship to the underlying harmony, it can be immensely helpful for the accompanist to provide sounds from the piano that help to entrain the harmonic rhythm and progression into the singer's mind and ear. We call these *harmonic entrainment devices*. The process of the first three readings of the piece includes a series of harmonic entrainment devices. Using repeated dominants is the best way to fine tune and polish intonation once a choir has gotten past those first three readings.

Repeated dominants, or "Tinkies," are used to help solidify a sense of harmonic progression and rhythm (*see Figure 12.4*). We take a unison octave (usually straddling the fifth and sixth, or sixth and seventh octaves of the piano) and play it as such:

Figure 12.4. Dominants, or "Tinkies."

The pitches we choose to use always relate to the harmonic structure of the piece we are accompanying. The octave is always split, with each note played as a subdivision of the underlying pulse.

This technique is used when the choir is experiencing intonation problems. Intonation problems usually occur for one of two common reasons: (1) vocal production issues or (2) an insufficient understanding of the harmonic progression/rhythm.

We supply dominants when we hear repeated intonation problems in a particular passage, not just when a previously unheard mistake is made. To begin, while the conductor rehearses the passage, we should accompany with dominants that change with each new chord the choir sings (*see Figure 12.5*).

Figure 12.5. Tinkies, local harmony.

Next, once the choir has properly tuned each chord individually, the choir must tune each chord to the harmonic progression. Consequently, we must determine the tonic or underlying tonal center of the passage and provide the related dominant (*see Figure 12.6*). For example:

Figure 12.6. Tinkies, greater harmony.

Using the dominants in this way gives the ear harmonic information that it needs to sing precisely the right pitches. We use a dominant because it signals to the choir which pitch, in the series of pitches that are being sung, is "Do." Using this tool only entrains a choir to better understand harmony. Additionally, I have found that this technique has a cumulatively positive effect on the choir. This technique encourages the choir to grow in its understanding of a piece's harmonic structure, as well as in its capacity to recognize harmonic progression and rhythm in pieces down the line.

AVOIDING TRICKY KEYS

Pieces that are written in C major or F major are notoriously difficult for choirs to tune. James Jordan and I will often move a piece up a half step or down a half step to overcome this challenge. Therefore, it is important that as accompanists we are prepared to meet this challenge and able to transpose up or down a half step on sight.

REFRESHING HARMONY

In the early stages of learning a piece, one of the trickiest things for a choir to manage is an unexpected or challenging key change or shift of tonal center. James Jordan and I have developed a number of different ways to handle these challenging moments. Even when a choir is very comfortable in their knowledge of the harmony, these moments can still be a challenge.

Stop and Start:

Figure 12.7. Stop and start.

- Accompanist plays final chord before tonal shift, followed by silence, followed by the next chord.

- Once the choir has heard this two or three times, they are instructed to do the same. The accompanist should play with them the first time, and then allow them to sing solo in the consecutive repetitions.

- Always play the chords as written (including thirds). The process here encourages the choir to first understand the harmony as it is tuned to the piano. Then, once the choir is comfortable with the harmony, it has the knowledge to sing solo and make the fine-tuned adjustments that are required for proper choral intonation.

Foreshadowing:

Figure 12.8. Foreshadowing, encourages choir
to audiate horizontally as well as vertically.

- As the choir approaches a harmonic shift, or a return to the tonic, the accompanist can use foreshadowing (*see Figure 12.8*) to help guide the ear to the next harmony.

- As the choir sings the chord immediately prior to the harmonic shift or return to tonic, the accompanist sounds "Do" in a low octave on the piano. The low octave can subtly guide the ear to the new tonal center, while not interrupting the sound the choir makes.

- Some composers even write this into their scores. Lauridsen's *O Nata Lux* contains a low octave in the piano (or orchestra), which apart from its musical intention, also serves to give the choir a unified "Do" to stand on.

OVERCOMING RHYTHMIC HURDLES

Rhythm can often be a challenge for any musician. Conductors often have choirs solve rhythmic problems by count singing, which entrains the choir to feel the subdivided, inner pulse within the macro beats. The same effect can be accomplished if the accompanist provides these subdivisions while the choir sings the music as written.

If the choir listens, and tracks the harmonic changes underneath them, then after two or three times, they will easily stand on their own. Count singing is still a very effective tool, but this alternative can be applied if count singing has not been enough to fix the problem or if the problematic section is very short.

The accompanist can simply provide this support, without anyone else thinking about it, and ensure that no singer learns this moment incorrectly (*see Figure 12.9*).

Figure 12.9. Rhythmic subdivisions.

COMMUNICATION

As musicians, we do not consider enough how communication works within a choir. Accompanists, in particular, have to ask:

- How do we communicate with the singers?
- What should we communicate to the singers?
- Do we ever communicate anything to the singers that we do not mean to?

Accompanists communicate more on our faces than we would ever realize that we do. Ambivalence, disappointment, surprise, contentment, joy, beauty—each of these emotions flicker across our faces even for just tiny moments in time. We should not hide these emotions; instead, we must be sure to communicate the reasons for these emotions to the appropriate individual.

In the rehearsal room at Westminster, there is an astounding amount of communication occurring. Yes, of course, the conductor is communicating both with words and gesture. As we have already learned, the accompanist is communicating greatly through the sound of the piano. Watching the choir, however, the observer can see that the sections are their own bustling beehives of communication. Singers are silently (and sometimes not so silently) communicating with each other. Section leaders are issuing instructions for re-voicings, colors, or techniques that will help meet the desires of the conductor. James Jordan even often defers to choir members to help diagnose and solve problems that occur.

I have found it particularly helpful to gain and maintain close working and personal relationships with section leaders. The Williamson Voices sections often have two section leaders, and from my position, I have a line of sight with all of them. Just a quick meeting of the eyes and a few exchanges of facial expressions between accompanist and section leader can communicate so much vital information:

- "I heard that, too. You should fix that in sectionals."
- "That fixed the problem."
- "Sorry that I just played the wrong note. You were right."
- "Listen to this!"

Never sacrifice your line of communication because you do not want to be a distraction or a nuisance. Use your instincts to avoid being a distraction or a nuisance, but if you, the accompanist, feel passionately about something, you must communicate that idea. If the section leader disagrees, then so be it. That is the worst that can happen. This level of communication facilitates highly ensemble-based singing and encourages the choir to sing with every ounce of musicianship it can muster.

WHERE'S MY TUXEDO?

All of the techniques that have been outlined thus far are applicable to both accompanied and unaccompanied music. You will have much more freedom and facility to apply these techniques in unaccompanied music, but when there are issues in accompanied music, you should be prepared to switch back and forth with ease, between a representation of the choral parts and a fully realized performance of your accompaniment.

Just like the conductor, who must think about process and product, the modern accompanist must be just as strong a performer as a pedagogue. It can feel odd to switch gears between the two, but our deep knowledge of a score that pedagogy demands can only go to strengthen the quality of our music making.

In my experience, the single most important skill of ensemble music making is listening. Many accompanists began their lives as solo pianists, adding accompanying out of desire or necessity. Solo pianists must also listen, but the listening is almost always audiating: hearing one's musical desires internally and allowing those musical desires to come to fruition through careful study and practice. The process becomes almost completely internalized.

In ensemble music making, I have always been told that it is essential to listen to others. It is true, without a doubt, that this makes such a difference. Everyone describes the sensation differently, but I know I am truly listening to my musical colleagues when I feel as if I can reach out and grasp the music in the air. We must also retain our ability to audiate like the solo pianist, while attentively listening to our musical colleagues. When we listen attentively to our fellow musicians, and they listen attentively to us, music becomes another language. No words need to be said—only rehearsal and experimentation with a healthy dose of imagination.

A FINAL NOTE: WARM-UPS

There are many texts already in existence that brilliantly tackle the challenge of accompanying warm-ups. Some conductors prefer unaccompanied warm-ups; others prefer slightly accompanied warm-ups, where the accompanist plays only the transpositions; and still others prefer fully accompanied warm-ups. James Jordan and Marilyn Shenenberger (my predecessor as James Jordan's accompanist) have collaborated previously to discuss and teach the art of accompanying warm-ups, including reasons for fully accompanying warm-ups. The text, The Choral Warm-Up Accompanist Supplement (GIA, is one of the best teaching tools on the subject.

It is worth mentioning, however, that the same topics we have examined previously also apply to our approach to accompanying warm-ups. We must consider how each warm-up, and each accompaniment, strengthens or changes the choir's sense of melody, harmony, rhythm, intonation, dynamics, and ensemble skills.

EPILOGUE:
THE FUTURE OF CHORAL MUSIC, CHORAL SINGING, AND WHY ALL OF THIS MATTERS

Most people would agree that much of the choral singing that occurs in the United States today occurs in and around universities. This is a good thing, in many ways. It ensures that writing, rehearsing, and performing choral music can be analyzed and understood thoroughly and academically. No longer is it acceptable to simply issue demands like, "Be better musicians!" or "That needs to be more in tune!" Instead, ensembles and their leaders are responsible for diagnosing, understanding, and solving problems that arise through the process of making music that changes someone's life.

This competency means that choral composers can be challenging, fresh, and idealistic about the works they create. Composers now have permission to stop asking, "What can't a choir do?" and start asking, "What *can* a choir do?" It is exciting and thrilling, and is only made possible by the fact that conductors study all elements of choral rehearsal and performance so deeply and intensely. It is not enough, however, to simply have the conductors understand these ideas. With the changes and growth that have occurred in the arts of choral composition and choral conducting, it has become clear that the choral accompanist can play a new, exciting, and challenging role as a musical leader equivalent to the conductor. Of course, the conductor must have final say on a few musical details. The process of building a composition from score to concert, however, now depends on teamwork. The modern choral accompanist, therefore, must seek the same knowledge as the conductor and, whenever possible, be able to translate this knowledge to the keyboard. Many conducting teachers have said that gesture must be a visual representation of sound. The goal of the modern choral accompanist, therefore, is to turn sound into gesture. With this mission, the accompanist and conductor can work totally complementary to each other, evoking only the best possible performances from the choirs with which they work.

CHAPTER 13
RE-LANGUAGING REHEARSALS

James Jordan

The conductor's opportunities for failure are so manifold that it scarcely is worth mentioning those of his collaborators. In the first place, it is the conductor's failure, if, by pre-rehearsal information and in-rehearsal procedures, he cannot produce performing skills which are accumulative, retentive—and, in the main, pleasurable. His also is the ultimate responsibility of transforming group lethargy and flaccidity to commitment and tonus. (p. 24)

—Robert Shaw
in *The Robert Shaw Reader*

The next chance you get to take part in any ensemble, notice the courage it takes to keep in tune with the ever-changing landscape of the music. We just don't play notes: music is a live current, and we navigate it. This current can be shaped and gently guided, but not pinned down. As players, we can influence its direction and add our personalities to the mix—but the moment we interfere too much, the music's power, effectiveness, and *flow* will be disturbed. If we are to master the power of the music as listeners and communicators, we have to be silent, attentive, and sensitive to its shape. We have to intuit a silent rhythm that has the power to unite us. We each have unique capacities to respond to music, and the better we understand, the more we feel, the closer we will come to the true spirit, and the more artistry we shall have to express. (p. 43)

—Barry Green
in *The Mastery of Music*

The assumption upon which all this increased pleasure is based you know probably as well as I. It is that a chorus is not a lump of human talent and energy chipped, sliced, rolled, molded and stamped into a maneuverable manikin of the lowest common artistic denominator, but a group of unique and varied human beings, voluntarily congregated, who accept personal responsibility, and bring to a performance of the whole each his utmost endowment, preparedness and sensitivity. Group productivity in art is not mass production. Art by the many, perhaps like government by the many, is at its best when it not only allows but also inspires the greatest possible individual participation, self-discipline, and self-expression. (p. 18)

—Robert Shaw
in *The Robert Shaw Reader*

What then are the *differences* between the choral and instrumental apparatuses?

The most apparent one is that, in general, the chorus deals with words, with human language, and the orchestra does not. In this respect *only*, the chorus is enormously more complex and complicated than the orchestra. Instruments initiate sounds by setting in motion vibrating surfaces or solids (percussion), vibrating columns of air (brass or winds) or vibrating strings (harp or violin). In each instance, the agent initiating the vibration is basically a very simple tool: a mallet for percussion, a vibrating reed or lip for winds, a taut and frictive ribbon or a plucking finger for the strings.

But, for a moment, bring to mind the size of the standard unabridged dictionary, and realize that, theoretically at least, it is conceivable that any first syllable in that dictionary could be asked to initiate a musical phrase, which could be followed by any other word forming unit at random *ad infinitum* and, further, assume that ours is a double chorus of eight parts, each with independent text, and that upon us rests the obligation of beginning together, proceeding together and ending together. It ain't easy. (pp. 384–385)

—Robert Shaw
in *The Robert Shaw Reader*

Convey the inner and hidden dialogue, the ying and the yang, the up and the down, the question and the answer, male and female, boy-girl, tension and relaxation. (p. 71)

Be considerate of the text. It just might coincide with melodic or harmonic accentuation—and this moment is the Pentecost of song. (p. 71)

Cultivate the forward look. Melody is a vagabond, incorrigibly searching the world for a place "really" to settle down. Even punctuation is not a period of retrospect, but of marshalling strength and scanning the horizon. The last note we sing is the one to which all others lead. (p. 71)

—Robert Shaw
in *The Robert Shaw Reader*

In *The Musician's Breath* (book and DVD), my co-author Nova Thomas speaks of the need to re-language the breath. I have come to understand that if one embraces this concept, and the philosophy as to why breath is important, then the paradigm of how we accomplish our musical objectives within a rehearsal must be altered somewhat radically. And our language that communicates a knowledge of the workings of the vocal mechanism are paramount to our work within the choral rehearsal.

Rehearsals are certainly a time for process. We must teach notes, rhythms, vocal techniques, and focus on elements of diction and color of language. But in the midst of all of this, I believe that we have not stitched together a rehearsal technique that not only introduces our singers to the power of the breath, but makes it the single most defining factor for realizing our own artistry. Whether it is an elementary choir, a high school ensemble, or a professional ensemble, our rehearsal process should always reflect the words of the old hymn tune, "Blest be the tie that binds." In a choral musician's world, it needs to become, "Blest be the breath that binds."

THE BINDING

This "binding" occurs through our suggestion that breath is the carrier of all ideas. This pedagogy demands that we elevate in our ensemble's mind that idea is breathed, and that the sound that follows will take care of itself. In a master class at Westminster, Thomas Hampson constantly reminded singers that you must tend to your technical details. But then, it is important to allow those technical details to be left alone to function as practiced so singers can focus on inhalation as being the uploading of all ideas that are about to be sung. I have found that this "binding" of breath to idea allows us to tap into the vast spiritual repository that grows out of our shared human experience.

THE LANGUAGE

It is all about language. First, you must tend to the technical details of mastering an understanding of breathing through the eight-handed breathing technique presented in Chapter 9. After the choir understands that process, then you must commit to what amounts to be almost a total psychological reconstruction of the inner dynamics of your choral rehearsal. Explain the breath and constantly reinforce it in daily rehearsal procedure as the carrier of human ideas.

Your choir must understand:

- That what you are attempting to develop is a parallel process to how you communicate verbally—that is, your breath on exhalation carries expression.

- That through your words, you somehow teach your choir to "trust" what you have rehearsed.

- That you and your choir must entrust their singing to the breath and *leave the musical line alone.* It is this concept that is the most difficult to grasp.

- That as conductor, you must, in your own spiritual equipment, allow yourself to place *all* trust in the breath and be a passionate advocate for your singers to do the same at every moment of their musicing.

- That your new process must constantly reinforce, cajole, and re-shape the creative mind of the choral singer to view the *BREATH* as *THE* most active time in the choral rehearsal.

- That you instill a passionate belief in your singers that breath is the only sure route into honest and authentic expression. That breath is the only way that ideas can be both visited and made apparent through the sounds being produced.

- That you finely tune your language in rehearsal to incite the creation of ideas. That you constantly use words to keep the ensemble focused on infusing idea into breath that then births sound.

- That rehearsals, ultimately, are about the breath and its empowerment.

- That rehearsals teach you, though this breath empowerment, to trust the music that is within you ready to be released.

- That you all become "explorers" of idea by probing the human meaning in texts; that exploration of the human ideas moves beyond mere translation of texts, but your study of texts reveals profound human truths and human meaning that then are entrusted to your breath through inhalation and exhalation.

- That you give a new, almost sacred reverence for the breath impulse gesture that precedes any musical phrase or beginning of a piece.

- That musical ideas are "uploaded" or "frontloaded" through the breath.

- That the breath becomes the forethought rather than the afterthought in the creative process.

- That both physical breath and idea are locked in a cyclic and ongoing process in musicing; that the understanding of the cyclic nature of breath provides for the constant nourishing of the sounds you sing *and* conduct.

- That this new focus on the miracles contained in the breath is a process of constant cultivation of both mind and the importance of birthing an idea.

- That the choral rehearsal teaches daily the sanctity of your individual ideas, and the integral importance of your individual ideas in the creation of a community of human expression that we have come to know as a choir.

- That you inspire daily and not be fearful of untrusting yourself as a conductor to the breath.

PART 4
THE HUMAN CONTENT OF TONE

CHAPTER 14
TEACHING WHAT IT IS TO LISTEN

James Jordan

Imagine how boring Jascha Heifetz would have been if only for a wonderful technician. He is a great violinist because he goes beyond the notes. For a singer, this is even more important, because we have words as well as notes. We must do everything an instrumentalist does plus more. It is very serious and difficult work, and it is not done out of bravura or by willpower alone, but out of love, a devotion to what you adore. This is the strongest reason for anything. (p. 4)

> —Maria Callas
>> in *Callas at Juilliard: The Master Classes*,
>> John Ardoin

There is something from the other side (of that painting) that comes through…but then I thought from the other side of what. Not the other side of the paper…but something from the other side of the senses that comes through is the way I put it. That's the only way I could account for what I was being filled with.

> —M. C. Richards
>> in *The Fire Within*

Rabbi Pinhas often cited the words: "A man's soul will teach him," and emphasized them by adding: "There is no man who is not constantly being taught by his soul." One of his disciples asked: "If this is so, why don't men obey their souls?" "The soul teaches constantly," Rabbi Pinhas explained, "but it never repeats." (p. 86)

> —Martin Buber
>> in *The Way of Man: Ten Rungs*

This book also attempts to create an awareness in conductors regarding tone that is informed by a listening sense that strives to "listen into" each sound the choir sings and to arrive at some opinion about the sacred and scientific alchemy that creates the magic of choral tone. The sonic content of any tone is part acoustic function of resonance. The other balancing part of choral tone is how that resonance is colored by human factors, which is deeply affected by the spiritual and human content of the breath that precedes any sung sound. But perhaps the single most important factor to deciphering the code of choral tone is one's ability to listen to choral sound in a deeply human and connected way.

The ability to listen in life is involuntary. We hear whether we want to or not. We do have the ability to selectively listen in life, and there begins the musician's downfall. We use this selective listening to handle the many "interferences" in our daily routine. This selective listening is the way we survive our daily routines. However, we must understand that listening to musical sounds requires a heightened sense of not only the sonic content of sound, but the human content that colors the sound.

If you use the analogy of a flickering flame, we might come closer to the challenge ahead of us. A scientist will tell you that it is impossible to describe either the size of a flame or its gaseous content because the flame flickers constantly. That flame has a direct relationship to the air that surrounds it. If one can fixate on a flame, its color and intensities are constantly in flux, all affected by the oxygen content of the air feeding that flame.

As a parallel, choral tone has many similarities to a flame. Choral tone is directly affected by breath. The color of sound is as elusive and changing as the colors within a flame. To see the color changes in the flame, one must stay in a connected visual relationship with the flame as it flickers and transforms itself. To accurately dissect and analyze elements of choral tone, one must activate through a voluntary act a deeper listening skill. Moving listening from an involuntary act to a deeply perceived and aware voluntary act is no small task. For most of us, it requires not only that we activate that deep inward listening, but also that listening must be prolonged throughout the duration of a phrase, an entire piece, or an entire rehearsal or performance.

To listen deeply is also a direct product of someone who wants to connect with others. There is no more profound human experience for a musician than the act of listening to others. In fact, for conductors, I believe it is *THE* skill that deepens the musicing act in conductors, but it is the single most important factor that affects the content of choral tone.

ESTABLISHING A PHILOSOPHICAL POINT OF VIEW

The audience of choral conductors and music educators (and possibly voice teachers) who read this book will have one of two perspectives. Many believe that tone production is mostly a scientific model, where one decides about how the tone should be built and balanced. Tone is, for the most part, a scientific and acoustic phenomenon that is highly specific and ordered. While the acoustic and vocal science aspects of tone are certainly realisms, this book will probably disappoint some who only view choral tone from this perspective.

The color of choral tone is directly influenced by human factors, and those factors cannot be underestimated in what becomes artistic product in sound. While one could manipulate tone into a resonential pocket, this book reinforces the fact that breadth of color—and more importantly, the human communicative value in tone—cannot and should not be underestimated. The acoustic properties of the singers' sound is directly related to the human component infused into the tone. The pedagogy must reflect a "head and heart" approach that builds tone from the inside out. The "interior" content of tone is the foundation upon which sounds sounded are made. Choral tone is a balancing act between acoustic and spirit, of which the latter perhaps is most important.

LISTENING TO CHORAL SOUND

My teacher, Elaine Brown, spoke on many occasions about listening and how important listening was for us as conductors and teachers. As conductors and teachers, we often admonish our groups to "Listen! Listen for details. The harmonic and melodic elements of the music must be accurate. Voices must be clear, beautiful, and well balanced."

Less often do conductors remember to say, "Listen! Listen to the composer of the musical details and to the author of the text. Listen to the spirit of these individuals and the ideas reflected in their music."

There is another kind of listening we should encourage in our singers, but we seldom do. We rarely say, "Listen! Listen to that which is best in yourselves." Why do we not provide for this ultimate "in-listening"? It must be either that we have not discovered the source of what brings out the best in ourselves, or that we are driven by the usual economic and schedule pressures involved in building a "successful" choir and we are afraid to make provision for listening in the deepest sense of the word.

There are two kinds of listening that become increasingly difficult to experience in the mad rush of everyday living. The first has to do with knowing how to be alone, how to listen long enough and carefully enough to our own thoughts until we father a series of tappings of our own inner resources. The second has to do with learning to listen to others, not just accommodatingly and passively, but to truly *LISTEN* to others.

Here and there, like a cry in the night, a thinking man is heard to say, "Stop right where you are and think! Listen while there is yet time." For the most part, this advice goes unheeded.

Can we teach our choirs, our classes, our music committees, and our boards of directors not only to provide for music performed, but through it, to relate to life itself? The supreme question in the minds of every one of us today is not how we can continue to survive, but how we can learn to live. This is what relating to life means. Musicians are not a special human brand of species who are exempt from concern and involvement. Unless they meet life where it touches them, their music will not ring true. It will be dull and flat. Might it not follow, then, that when music making precedes action, it begins to approach the ultimate in beauty and truth?

As Edna St. Vincent Millay noted in one of her poems:

> The World stands out on either side
> No wider than the heart is wide;
> Above the world reaches the sky
> No higher than the soul is high.
> The heart can push the sea and land
> Farther apart on either hand;
> The soul can split the sky in two
> And let the face of God shine through;
> But east and west will crush the heart
> That cannot keep them pushed apart,
> And he whose soul is flat, the sky
> Will cave in on him by and by...[29]

The voluntary listening described above is very different from what I have labeled as *involuntary listening*. Voluntary listening is analogous to an aural

---

29 James Jordan, *Lighting a Candle* (Chicago: GIA, 2013).

microscope. When one uses a microscope, one may adjust that microscope to view the larger scheme of things, or one may adjust that microscope downward to probe the deeply interior structure of a cell. As conductors, we must develop a listening "microscope" that deepens the levels at which we hear, exposing to us the very sonic content of the tone. Hearing that tone is one challenge. Analyzing that tone in the moment is a direct by-product of wanting to hear certain contents of that tone.

THE SIX LAYERS OF VOLUNTARY LISTENING

For me, the content of what should be heard exists within a six-layered texture:

1. The human content of tone
2. The resonance content of the tone
3. The vocal health of the tone
4. The anatomy of the breath that precedes the sound
5. The intonation of the pitch as it relates to the harmonic structure
6. The Life of the tone, or its morphology, as it lives its life from beginning to end, embedded within the harmonic rhythm of the work.

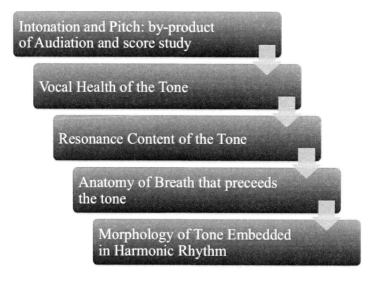

Figure 15.1. Levels of voluntary listening.

Each of these levels comprises a deepening depth of listening. Some conductors exist in only one of these levels. Others exist in two or more. I have found that those types of listeners are for the most part "involuntary" and generally focus their rehearsal or conducting process on teaching rather than listening. Listening is a micro event that focuses on a proper "correction" of an immediate problem, usually pitch and rhythm. In many cases, one's listening world is locked there and very rarely, if ever, journeys out of that realm. Young conductors are especially vulnerable to this somewhat myopic approach to listening.

THE CHALLENGE OF "LISTENING INTO" SOUND

In a quote that begins this chapter, M. C. Richards talks of seeing through the colors of the painting to what is beyond or behind the colors that meet our eyes. I am beginning to believe that I was indeed fortunate to have had teachers who always taught me in some way to listen "into" the sound. A simple parallel analogy would be to ask yourself this question: Can you hear "human" and "emotional" and even the spiritual content in one's speaking voice? I think most of us would answer that we can if we choose to be listening in a way that allows us to hear "inside" the sound or beneath the surface of the grammar and the syntax of what is being spoken. In music, the ability to hear "below the surface" of the sound is a skill that both teachers and conductors must develop to a very high level.

All of my teachers forced me, in many different ways, to hear things that were beyond the pitches, the rhythm, and the textural clarity of the work at hand. Hearing what is human and expressive in a sound has always been at the forefront of any rehearsing or conducting that I do. Even after thirty years as a conductor, I do not claim to fully understand what all this "inner listening" is comprised of. But I do know that if we want our ensembles to be expressive, somehow, we must move ourselves to higher ground that moves musical sound from mundane and "clean" to a level that communicates, soul to soul, at a deep level.

QUALITIES OF THE SOUND BENEATH THE SURFACE

The qualities of the "sound beneath the surface" can be labeled for the purposes of this discussion as *honest and vulnerable*. Sound, I believe, can and does carry deep messages within its sonorance, if permitted. Resonances that are brilliant have a brilliance because the human spirit provides the "stuff" into such sounds. The vulnerability that is fostered and engendered by trust has a singularly unique color that can be heard.

As conductors and teachers, we must understand that sound must be allowed to have a life of its own—not restricted or confined to an acoustic box. To confine sound is to confine both soul and spirit. Sound restricted by technical confines places borders on human expressivity. Certainly, there are parameters that must be defined, but those parameters must not, unknowingly or unwillingly, restrict the sound of the spirit.

Vulnerability is a specific quality in musical sound. Musicians must want to hear it just in the same way they want to hear it in meaningful everyday conversation. Vulnerable sound is luminescent…deeply compelling, impassioned, roundly resonant, soul warming, and humanly vibrant. Musical sound thatched with vulnerability draws us in. Its seductive qualities draw our ears toward it. Vulnerable sound does not allow for mere monitoring; it draws us inward, profoundly inward.

Expectation and standards of expectation are everything, I believe, in this somewhat mystical process. We must each set a standard by which we are deeply vigilant to hear these mystical qualities in musical sound. We must be careful that we become aware when we are seduced *only* by correct pitch, correct rhythm, correct articulation, correct vowels. These are the aural representations of the color in a painting that M. C. Richards speaks of above. If we let down our standards, we set a lower expectation for our own inner listening sense and, thus, a lower standard from the ensemble, which can and is perceived wordlessly by the ensemble. To hear at this deep level, the lesson I have been taught is that our ears can only be opened by vulnerability tempered with a great deal of love. The alchemy of these two elements is one of the most powerful antidote for not just opening one's ears, but throwing open the doors of one's spirit to listen and communicate the deepest aspects of human experience. We become handicapped, in a sense, by our own neurology. Sheer human will can bypass the default in all of us, which allows us to say, as my teacher Elaine Brown used to say daily, "We hear, but we do not really listen."

The left hemisphere is specialized not only for the actual production of speech sounds, but for the imposition of syntactic structure on speech for what is called *semantics*—comprehension of meaning. The right hemisphere, on the other hand, does not govern spoken words, but seems to be concerned with more subtle aspects of the language, such as nuances of metaphor, allegory, and ambiguity—skills that are inadequately emphasized in our elementary schools but that are vital for the advance of civilizations through poetry, myth, and drama. We tend to call the left the major or "dominant" hemisphere because it, like a chauvinist, does all the talking (and maybe too much of the internal thinking as well), claiming to be the repository of humanity's highest attribute, language. Unfortunately, the mute right hemisphere can do nothing to protest. (p. 133)

—V. S. Ramachandran
in *Phantoms in the Brain*

While the quote above may delineate the neurological challenges of listening in a deeper way, it does not identify those things that might "close the door" to our own ability as artists to hear meaning and honesty in sound at a deeper level. The ability to listen at the deepest level is intimately tied to our ability to be truly vulnerable "in public." This ability to "open oneself" is both an acquired skill and an acquired taste. Vulnerability in public can, at first blush, be deeply uncomfortable and even frightening until vulnerability becomes your friend, a safe partner in the musicing process.

CHAPTER 15
SACRED SINGING SPACE

James Jordan

With every class, her classroom was a sacred space….

> —Bradley Cooper
> in *Inside the Actor's Studio*
> with James Lipton, March 15, 2011

I hope they are as human as they sound. (p. 36)

> —Dr. Bonnell,
> The Invasion of the Body Snatchers
> in Kathleen Marie Higgins,
> *The Music Between Us*

Toward the end of the process—having held the bird with the best of intentions—we may find our cupped hands making a subtle but persistent upward motion, encouraging the bird to fly. "Don't you see what you have learned here? Aren't you ready to take off, to act on what you now know?" Resist the temptation to. The bird will fly when it is ready, and we cannot possibly know when that will be. (p. 146)

But exactly how solitude and community go together turns out to be trickier than breathing. We say we are in solitude, we often bring other people with us: think of how often our "solitude" is interrupted by an interior conversation with someone who is not there! When we say we are in community, we often lose track of true self: think of how easily we can forget who we are when we get entangled in group dynamics.

If we are to hold solitude and community together as a true paradox, we need to deepen our understanding of both poles. *Solitude* does not necessarily mean living apart from others; rather it means never living apart from one's self. It is not about the absence of other people—it is about being fully present to ourselves, whether or not we are with others. Community does not necessarily mean coming face to face with others; rather it means never losing the awareness that we are connected to each other. It is not about the presence of other people—it is about being fully open to the reality of relationship, whether or not we are alone. (p. 55)

—Parker Palmer
in *A Hidden Wholeness*

We must learn to know ourselves better through art. We must rely more on the unconscious, inspirational side of man. We must not enslave ourselves to dogma. We must believe in the attainability of good. We must believe, without fear, in people. (p. 21)

—Leonard Bernstein
in *This I Believe*

Yes, there's an inner geography of the human being that can be captured by music, and not by anything else. That's the real magic of music, and that's why Walter Pater said that "all art aspires toward conditions of music." … and that accounts for James Joyce and Gerard Manley Hopkins and Keats and Shakespeare and Holderin, or for a diagonal in a Cimabue Madonna—the thing that makes you gasp when you look at this picture. There's something that is echoing an inner geography inside you, and you *feel* it…as in the Schubert Trio, in *Tristan*….

—Leonard Bernstein
in Jonathan Cott, *Dinner with Lenny*

Sometimes I think I am a slow learner regarding the most important issues revolving around our choral art. I really can't blame my teachers. And I certainly can't blame my students. What I can blame is my inability to hear and feel the obvious when my pedagogical brain overtakes my best teaching senses. The major tenet of this book is to try to re-shape and re-focus choral pedagogy, and in essence, re-prioritize what should be important to all of us as we work with our choirs.

Experience is always the best teacher if we are willing to understand what we hear and experience. Much of my professional life has been spent studying pedagogy—how people learn music. I have had the distinct honor of studying with one of the great pedagogical minds of music education, Edwin Gordon. I know how easy it is to continually focus on pedagogy. Teaching technique rooted in a consistent pedagogy can serve as a conductor's "comfort food." There *is* a good feeling when we teach something well. There *is* a good feeling when we believe that we are "improving the skills" of the singers in our ensemble. Such achievement provides a "false mask" of sorts that musicing in the ensemble is moving forward and to higher ground. The sounding of the music certainly does improve, but does the music really improve? If we are very honest, and we listen to what is being sounded by the ensemble, we will hear the sound as being devoid of properties that are usually associated with music as art that speaks directly into the spiritual core of people and, consequently, becomes transformative.

MUSIC AS TRANSFORMATION

Transformative music experiences are deeply life changing, but they are not so much about technique as they are about the spirit contained in a community of people. How do I know this? After over thirty years of teaching "technique" and having a deep and abiding passion about pedagogy, I have learned that we must navigate our way through the thicket of pedagogy into a clearing of sorts where we can step back and understand that *only community can enable any pedagogy.* Our pedagogy and skill will be continually undermined unless we respect the power of community to achieve and teach things that we cannot learn as meaningfully on our own as we can within a deeply connected community of people functioning as a choral ensemble. Pedagogically, we as conductors and teachers have not exercised due diligence in studying the "psychology of community" that can be grown within every choral ensemble. If we allow community to take root rather than throwing interference passes with pedagogical minutiae, we will find that the "art" and honesty of the sound within the choral ensemble will grow exponentially.

Yes, I am a slow learner, but I have grown enough as a conductor to become a somewhat skilled observer of what is happening in front of me. For me, rehearsal technique is not so much any more about pedagogical processes (although that is important), but more about keeping a watchful eye on the human content of the ensemble and making note when the honesty of the sound I hear takes a quantum leap before my "ears."

THE OXFORD EXPERIENCE

One is certainly shaped by one's experience. Often when experiences are powerful, one is deeply affected in the moment and then is forced to explain, after the fact, what has happened.

In 2013, we began a program at Westminster, The Choral Institute at Oxford. This program was developed in partnership with St. Stephen's House, a

Hall of the University at Oxford. The objective was naively simple in my mind: to build an exemplary conducting program where there would be an "ensemble in residence" of the highest level so conductors could use sound as their teacher and not hide behind teaching. The "hiding behind pedagogy" gets in the way of the art and magic of what we are attempting to do in a choral rehearsal. However, what we all witnessed has shaken my pedagogical roots and re-planted them in new, fresh soil, in the very place that my teacher, Elaine Brown, tried to do some thirty years ago. While I always believed on an intellectual level that there was both pedagogical and human truth in what Elaine Brown tried to teach us, it is only because of Oxford that I now can say I understand because I have experienced it in both sound and human connection.

No explanation of this experience can do it justice, but I will try to explain in the best way I can why this singular experience has re-focused my teaching and re-aligned by ideas about how one "builds" a choral tone. So, the Oxford program began with twenty eager conductors and a choir in residence that had sung together beautifully all year. We were all gathered together at St. Stephen's in Oxford, a monastic structure complete with private chapels, classroom, and cloisters. Because we were in Oxford, we had afternoon tea and Evening Compline. As a sort of orientation, the choir and conductors learned how to sing an Evening Compline service. For those of you who are unfamiliar with the Office of the Day, it consists of a beautiful sequence of monophonic chants sung by the entire community in alternation. We all ended our day in a spiritual place singing together. But what happened during the course of this program revealed in a brilliant way how choral music can transform people through the sounds we sing. Because there was no pedagogy (i.e., rehearsal technique talked or dwelled upon), the focus, accidentally, was upon sound. Because of the sacred place we occupied, the Williamson Voices, the choir in residence, magically grew closer. They gave to each conductor in such profoundly moving ways through both their singing and their emotional support that, through sound, they empowered both the music and *each* conductor. The community that was that choir has now re-focused me regarding the impact community has upon both tone and technique. Imagine, not one word of technical information was discussed in ten days! It was the silent power of that community and its growth within that enabled the growth in those conductors *AND* gave the music we sang a compelling and deeply honest voice beyond what I ever envisioned possible.

POSSIBLE EXPLANATIONS

Using the Oxford experience as a "teachable moment," if we step away and try to analyze what happened to all of us, conclusions appear clearly. The basic ingredients were:

1. A resident choral ensemble that had established strong connections with each other through the music they made together;

2. The desire for the ensemble to share those connections with others;

3. Conductors who allowed themselves to be somewhat vulnerable, and that vulnerability was coaxed out of them by a caring ensemble;

4. The choir, somehow, made each conductor a sense of belonging; and

5. The product of the choir's openness and the conductor's desire to grow caused conductors to embrace their vulnerability in this safe place.

Further, the normal "numbing" that I believe happens in conductors (specifically a numbing toward listening and hearing *into* the sound, a numbing of self, and a numbing of human connection) did not exist in this situation. Using the framework that is suggested by Brene Brown (*see Figure 16.1*),[30] everyone's growth can be measured by these very specific criteria:

Sensing Love and Belonging:
Essential Elements of Connection

1. Sense of courage – the courage to be imperfect
2. Compassion to be kind to selves and others
3. Have a sense of authenticity that is connection

---

30 I am grateful to Dr. Brown's paradigm and words to describe what is difficult, at best, to describe— that is, those elements that might define vulnerability and our ability to access a vulnerable place. In music, I believe that the challenge may be greater because of the collision of both human interactions and musical interactions, especially as we conduct and attempt connection with others.

4. Fully embraced vulnerability[31]
5. Vulnerability of the birthplace of joy, creation, magic
6. Do not numb vulnerability
7. Numbing knows no specifics...numbing infects everything
8. We tend to perfect....and that doesn't accomplish anything
9. Worthy of love and belonging
10. We pretend that what we do does not have an impact on people!
11. Let yourself be SEEN!! Practice gratitude and joy.
12. Believe that you are enough.

Figure 16.1. Suggested framework by Brene Brown.

AN ANALYSIS OF PORTALS FOR VULNERABILITY AND CONNECTEDNESS

There is something strange about the range of actions mirror neurons respond to. They don't respond to pantomimes or meaningless gestures or to random animal sounds. They seem specially tuned to respond to actions with clear goals—whether those actions are perceived through sight, sound, or any sensory pathway.

—Ben Thomas
in "What's So Special About Mirror Neurons?"
Scientific American (November 6, 2012)

Examining the list above, I would like to apply these principles to the Oxford experience as a possible paradigm for rehearsals and performances with our ensembles. In all cases, directly, or indirectly, these interactions profoundly influence the spiritual content of choral tone.

Important to this discussion, and perhaps all of the discussions in this book, is the information we are gaining from studying the activity of mirror neurons. It is clear that the channel for connectedness and communication not only lies deep within our neurology, but also that mirror neurons play a significant role in the depth of what we share with others and has much to do with how all things human are shared with others. Vulnerability alone cannot be communicated in the ways that affect choral tone without some alive "pathway" for those very strong human impulses to travel. Again, using the Oxford experience, let me try to distill that experience into some things that might help to nourish the choral tone of our ensembles in a deeply meaningful way.

---

31 The lectures and writings of Brene Brown shed light on the essentials of connection within this situation.

SENSE OF COURAGE – THE COURAGE TO BE IMPERFECT

In hindsight, the courage to be imperfect was nurtured by the "sacred place" that was created by both the architecture of St. Stephen's Hall, a historically monastic place, and the "sacred space" that was clearly established within the choir and without. To take the chance to be imperfect, we must be able to feel as if we are in a "safe" place. And we must accept that "mistakes" can be made and that we can grow because of them—because of the environment. Imperfection is part of art…and imperfection can truly be our teacher. If the human situation allows for it, then amazing growth and listening are the result. One of the problems we have as conductors is that we are afraid to hear imperfection. Not only are we afraid to hear imperfection, but we are afraid to accept responsibility for it, in some way. Acknowledging that the sound can improve and that we can make that "imperfection" go away is part of our journey, and it has everything to do with the anatomy of a choral tone sounded.

COMPASSION TO BE KIND TO SELVES AND OTHERS

Kindness, without doubt, is a way inward—a way inward to a much deeper place. In *The Musician's Soul,* I wrote about mimetics, which revolves around our human need to envy others and not love ourselves. We must live compassionately with ourselves; but also, ensembles who sing must adopt compassion as the way of "doing musical business." Perhaps no other human characteristic can be heard within a "sleeve" of choral tone than when singers are singing the tone root within a compassionate and deeply caring being. Kindness must be all around, in every word spoken and in every action entered into. And this, I have learned, is a wide two-way street for both conductor and singer.

HAVE A SENSE OF AUTHENTICITY THAT IS CONNECTION

We must want a connection with others to have one. To merely acknowledge that connection is important is not sufficient. For me, authenticity of self rests in a deeply honest desire to want to share with others in the most deeply human way possible. Singers can sense immediately inauthenticity and music making that doesn't go much below the human surface of things. If we genuinely want connection, and we have reflected, and we are able to place ourselves in a place inside of ourselves that is authentic, then connection begins and is nourished. Acknowledging that connection is the goal will never achieve it. Connection is a deep journey inward that identifies a place from which our musical work must be done in every rehearsal and every concert. This place, once identified, must be our continual refuge, which is then reflected in the tone and human content of that tone.

FULLY EMBRACED VULNERABILITY

Part of the challenge we face is that we must acknowledge that the inherent color of choral tone is a reflection of that inner space spoken of above. Once we identify that inner place of "connection" that is continually nurtured through a sense of self-love, we can begin to "embrace" this new location for music making with excitement and a new sense of exploration. Vulnerability, actually, is a place of great security when it is identified as such. We avoid vulnerability and its sensation within because we have associated it with negative reinforcement and an "unsafe" place. It is exactly the opposite. Embracing vulnerability within ourselves enables us to open a communicative channel with singers that not only allows them to sing, but also gives them "permission" to be vulnerable themselves, especially in an ensemble. This is due to the fact that they feel as if they are in a "safe" place.

VULNERABILITY OF THE BIRTHPLACE OF JOY, CREATION, MAGIC

If we listen to the sounds that come from singers when the above is in place, we can begin to hear a world of sound open in front of us. We begin to understand that our gesture can birth magic in all its dimensions. That tone that truly carries joy has a distinct resonance to it that defies a type of music contrivance or manipulation by either conductor or singer. We become empowered, in a way, because of the "sacred place" where we are not afraid of the newness of sounds, but we seek out those new sounds in every rehearsal and every performance.

DO NOT NUMB VULNERABILITY

Our human tendency is to numb vulnerability to the point where we believe that vulnerability *is* that feeling of numbness. Numbing deep human feeling and awareness can become the norm in musicians if we are not careful. A numbed sense of vulnerability, visited day in and day out, becomes what we believe vulnerability to be. Non-numbed vulnerability is birthed in a place that is "relaxed" within us. We must be "relaxed" to feel vulnerability—or anything, for that matter! I learned through the Oxford experience that it was that place, those people, that allowed for conductors to "relax" into the place where they feel vulnerability in its truest and most authentic place.

> Recognize what is before your eyes, and what is hidden will be revealed to you. (p. 201)
>
> —The Gospel of Thomas
> in Thomas Moore, *Care of the Soul*

> Hearing something new is embarrassing and difficulty for the ear; foreign music we do not hear well. (p. 55)
>
> —Friedrich Nietzche,
> *Beyond Good and Evil*

CHAPTER 16

HARMONIC RHYTHM UNDERSTANDING AND ITS BINDING RELATIONSHIP TO BREATH

James Jordan

Three forces are at work in chord-connection: rhythmic, melodic, and harmonic. Each of them works in two directions. Rhythm determines the duration of the chords, and groups them by division into stressed and unstressed members of the structure. Melody in voice leading regulates linear expansion, and in the two-voice framework sets pitch limits. In placing the harmonic center of gravity and in the regulation of relationships we see harmonic energy at work. (p. 109)

—Paul Hindemith
in *The Craft of Musical Composition,*
Book 1: Theory

The rhythm texture of music…In its total effect on the listener, the rhythm of music derives from two main sources, melodic and harmonic. (p. 123)

It is assumed that the conceptions meter and rhythm are understood. Meter is simply measure. Meter has no rhythm. But music so often has a rhythmic pulse with which meter coincides at important points that we think the meter is rhythmic. We then speak of strong and weak beats of the measures, forgetting that the rhythm of the music came first, and that afterwards came the effort to place the bar-line at the points of rhythmic stress. Obviously, the first beat of the measure should receive rhythmic stress only when the music calls for it, and not because it happens to be the first beat. (p. 121)

The harmonic rhythm, that is to say, the distribution of chord changes in the phrase, is of great importance in the structure. This principle should be the subject of extensive research during the study of harmony, to bring out the great diversity of effect achieved by harmonic means. (p. 61)

—Walter Piston
in *Harmony*

H*armonic rhythm* is a term that has fallen out of favor in past decades. If we begin with the assumption that a definition of music is one that defines music as sound moving forward, then some definition is needed to quantify and describe this concept. It is clear from the writings of my colleagues, Sean McCarther and Kathy Price, that breath is the fuel by which resonances are transformed to singing.

It has come to me at this point in my career that in order for sound to move forward, breath must constantly move forward. No breath equals no line and certainly no resonance. So, for me, a new passion has taken over my own pedagogy that focuses on active inhalation that is in the spirit and meaning of the music along with a gesture that reflects and mirrors the harmonic rhythm of the work I am conducting.

Pure and simple, harmonic rhythm is defined as the rate of speed that sound moves forward. In reading the quote by composer/theorist Walter Piston at the beginning of this chapter, we find the historic beginnings of the actual definition of harmonic rhythm. The rate of perceived speed of sound moving forward is certainly a subjective perception. From this author's point of view, it is the harmonic rhythm that informs musicians of the overall architecture or overall arch of the musical phrase.

It also follows, then, that if we perceive the speed of the sound moving forward, then we are provided with information by the composer on the speed of air necessary to move vocal resonance (singing) forward. For conductors and singers, sound moving forward must be a deeply felt kinesthetic act. In fact, there is nothing more important to expressive, honest musicianship than the constant awareness of just how fast sound is moving forward.

Harmonic rhythm has a parallel analogy in language to the speaking of complete, emotion-ladened expressive ideas in complete sentences, even paragraphs. Harmonic progression truly must be at the foundation of how we move as conductors and how we breathe as singers. To borrow an analogy from Sean McCarther, breath is the gas pedal for our vocal car. If we let up on the "air pedal," we have less sound and less forward movement. Our breath pedal must always be down when singing. The development of this "bonding" of kinesthesia to harmonic progression must be our goal in the choral rehearsal. An intimate awareness of the magnetism and allure of harmonic progression should be the foundation of our pedagogical craft. Put more directly, voice science has pointed a clear direction for choral conductors to not only understand voice science, but to conduct in empathy with that science. So in many ways, this chapter is the logical gestural and pedagogical conclusion to this book.

THE TRAUMA OF WEIGHT UPON THE VOICE

It is no over-dramatization to use the word "trauma" in the heading for this section. My more recent revelation in *Discovering Chant* (GIA, 2014) presents the use of chant as a pedagogical tool and the wisdom contained within the correct performance practice of chant—that weight damages musical expression and also "puts the breaks" on the forward movement of sound, which handicaps the movement of air to allow the voice to function in a free and expressive manner. Many conductors apply weight somewhat consistently, and at times violently on the beat after each bar line. The immediate effect is slowing of the forward movement of air and, consequently, sound. But the other toxic effect is the wordless control that is displaced onto the beat, which in turn, traumatizes the larynx by the abrupt adjustment in the forward movement of the air. The effects of this weight are many, and they are not positive. Musical line that is breath-fed is never served by this displacement of weight. The forward movement of sound is only served by attention to the inner parts of the bar.

INNER-BAR PHRASE DIRECTION

Almost without exception, if we listen to the forward movement of harmonic rhythm, we will hear that most, if not all, of the propelling, forward-moving harmonic velocity occurs in the middle parts of the bar—that is, in 4/4 the momentum occurs on beats 2 and 3; and in 3/4 the momentum and harmonic activity occurs on beat 2. It is in those beats where the energy and movement of the singers' breath must be supported by the conductor's gesture, and that speed must never be slowed by undue weight applied onto the first beat of the bar either by the singers or the conductor. Perhaps more than any other factor, the forward movement of the breath and its bound relationship with the harmonic rhythm of the phrase has everything to do with the forward movement of the sound and the arching architecture of the very phrase itself. Harmonic rhythm and breath are intimately connected to each other. It is our role as conductors to empathize at all times with the harmonic rhythm through gestures that support and mirror the forward movement of both sound and air. Weight is the enemy of all these things, not to mention the control that is implicitly implied by conductors who use weight as a habit rather than as a factor that is used sparingly. There is a movement kinesthetic that is surprisingly different for conductors when they "conduct" the perceived speed of the harmonic rhythm.

THE RELEASE CONTAINED WITHIN GESTURE

There is another fact other than weight that can sabotage the singers' breath. The term *rebound* is used to commonly refer to the "up" part of the beat. In most cases, the speed or the velocity of that rebound is never discussed, and its feeling kinesthetic is never examined. For singers to use breath that creates resonance, we must at all times treat the rebound of each beat as a release! When conducting, we should "let go" of the sound after the ictus. By decelerating the rebound, or letting go of the control of the upward beat, we empower singers to take responsibility for their own breath movement (that is determined by the speed of the harmonic rhythm). There perhaps is nothing more important for us to understand as conductors to allow for all miracles of the voice to happen as discussed earlier in this book. It is always about the release in our gesture that allows singers to move their breath in a way that is empathetic to the healthy functioning of the singing voice.

THE ROLE OF BREATH

Finally, it *IS* all about the breath. To believe that breath carries meaning is the be all and end all of great choral singing. The conductor's initiating, impelling breath sets an instinctive pattern within the singers that immediately connects conductor to both breath and tone. Mastery of breathing, perception of harmonic rhythm, understanding of the negative factors that gestural weight introduces into singers—these are the keys to all things musical. We have much to learn from our voice science, keyboard, and vocal coach colleagues. All of it is unified and made whole by an awareness of breath and our willingness to connect to the harmonic rhythm of any phrase. When these factors are married, spontaneous, honest music making can be the only possible result.

BIBLIOGRAPHY AND RESOURCE LIST

Aaron, J. "A study of the effects of vocal coordination on pitch accuracy, range, pitch discrimination, and tonal memory of inaccurate singers." Ph.D. dissertation. The University of Iowa, 1990.

Adler, Kurt. *Phonetics and Diction in Singing.* Minneapolis, MN: University of Minnesota Press, 1967.

Agostini, Emilo. "Diaphragm Activity in Breath Holding: Factors Relating to Onset." *Journal of Applied Physiology,* 18, 1963, pp. 30-36.

Andrews, Moya L., and Anne C. Summers. *Voice Therapy for Adolescents.* San Diego, CA: Singular Publishing Group, 1991.

Appelman, D. Ralph. "Science of Resonance," *Music Journal,* 17, 1959, pp. 44-45.

———. *The Science of Vocal Pedagogy.* Bloomington, IN: Indiana University Press, 1967.

Archibeque, Charlene. "Making Rehearsal Time Count." *The Choral Journal,* September 1992, pp. 18-19.

Armstrong, Kerchal, and Donald Hustad. *Choral Musicianship and Voice Training: An Introduction.* Carol Stream, IL: Somerset Press, 1986.

Baer, Hermanus. "Establishing a Correct Basic Technique for Singing." *The NATS Bulletin,* 28, 1972, pp. 12-14.

Baldwin, James. "Some Techniques for Achieving Better Choral Tone Through Vowel Purity." *The Choral Journal,* September 1985, pp. 5-12.

Barlow, W. *The Alexander Technique.* New York: Alfred A Knopf, 1973.

Bartle, Jean Ashworth. *Lifeline for Children's Choir Directors.* Toronto: Gordon V. Thompson, 1988.

Bassini, Carlo. *Bassini's Art of Singing: An Analytical and Physiological*

System for the Cultivation of the Voice. Boston, MA: Oliver Ditson and Co., 1857.

Bergman, Leola Nelson. *Music Master of the Middle West: The Story of F. Melius Christiansen and the St. Olaf Choir.* New York: Da Capo Press, 1968.

Bertalot, John. *5 Wheels to Successful Sight Reading.* Minneapolis, MN: Augsburg Fortress, 1993.

———. *Immediately Practical Tips for Choral Directors.* Minneapolis, MN: Augsburg Fortress, 2003.

Bertaux, B. "Teaching Children of All Ages to Use the Singing Voice" and "How to Work with Out-of-Tune Singers." In Darrel Walters and Cynthia Taggart, *Readings in Music Learning Theory.* Chicago: GIA Publications, pp. 92-104.

Blackstone, Jerry. *Working with Male Voices.* (Video) Santa Barbara, CA: Santa Barbara Music.

Bloom, Benjamin. *Stability and Change in Human Characteristics.* New York: Wiley, 1964.

Bollew, Jospeh A. "Is Falsetto False?" *The Etude,* July 1954, p. 14.

Boone, D.R. *The Voice and Voice Therapy.* Englewood Cliffs, NJ, Prentice-Hall, 1977.

Bouhuys, Arend. *The Physiology of Breathing.* London: Gruene and Stratton, 1977.

Bradley, M. "Prevention and Correction of Vocal Disorders in Singers." *The NATS Bulletin,* May/June 1980, p.39.

Bravender, Paul E. "The Effect of Cheerleading on the Female Singing Voice." *The NATS Bulletin,* 37, 1980, p. 39.

Brodnitz, Friederich. "On Change of Voice." *The NATS Bulletin,* 40, 1984, pp. 24-26.

Brown, Ralph Morse. *The Singing Voice.* New York: Macmillan Co., 1946.

Brown, William Earl. *Vocal Wisdom: Maxims of Giovanni Battista Lamperti.* Enlarged Edition. Boston, MA: Crescendo Publishers, 1973.

Bunch, Meribeth. *Dynamics of the Singing Voice.* New York: Springer-Verlag, 1982.

Burgin, John Carroll. *Teaching Singing.* Metuchen, NJ: Scarecrow Press, 1973.

Campbell, Don G. *Master Teacher: Nadia Boulanger.* Washington, DC: The Pastoral Press, 1984.

Christy, Van A. *Expressive Singing.* Dubuque, IA: William C. Brown and Co., 1974.

———. *Foundations in Singing.* Dubuque, IA: William C. Brown and Co., 1976.

Clippinger, David Alva. *The Head Voice and Other Problems.* Boston, MA: Oliver Ditson, 1917.

Coffin, Berton. "The Instrumental Resonance of the Singing Voice." *The NATS Bulletin,* 31, 1974, pp. 26-39.

———. "The Relationship of Breath, Phonation and Resonance in Singing." *The NATS Bulletin,* 31, 1975, pp. 18-24.

Collins, D.L. *The Cambiata Concept.* Arkansas: The Cambiata Press, 1981.

Colwell, Richard. *The Evaluation of Music Teaching Learning.* Englewood Cliffs, NJ: Prentice-Hall, 1970.

Cooksey, John M. "Development of a Contemporary, Eclectic Theory for the Training and Cultivation of the Junior High School Male Changing Voice. *The Choral Journal,* 18, October 1977 and January 1978.

———. "Development of a Contemporary, Eclectic Theory for the Training and Cultivation of the High School Male Changing Voice." *The Choral Journal,* October 1977.

———. "Development of a Contemporary, Eclectic Theory for the Training and Cultivation of the High School Male Changing Voice: Part II: Scientific and Empirical Findings; Some Tentative Solutions." *The Choral Journal,* October 1977, pp. 12-14.

———. " Development of a Contemporary, Eclectic Theory for the Training and Cultivation of the High School Male Changing Voice: Part III: Developing an Integrated Approach to the Care and Training of the Junior High School Male Changing Voice." *The Choral Journal,* October 1977, pp. 7-9.

———. *Working with Adolescent Voices.* St. Louis, MO: CPH, 1999.

Cooper, Morton. "Vocal Suicide in Singers." *The NATS Bulletin,* 16, 1970, p. 31.

Corbin, Lynn A. "Practical Applications of Vocal Pedagogy for Choral Ensembles." *The Choral Journal,* March 1986, pp. 5-10.

Cott, Jonathan. *Dinner with Lenny.* New York: Oxford University Press, 2013.

Coward, Henry. *Choral Technique and Interpretation.* Salem, NH: Ayer Company Publishers, 1972.

Dart, Thurston. *The Interpretation of Music.* New York: Harper and Row, 1963.

Darrow, G.F. *Four Decades of Choral Training.* Metuchen, NJ: The Scarecrow Press, 1975.

Davison, Archibald T. *Choral Conducting.* Cambridge, MA: Harvard University Press, 1940.

Decker, Harold A., and Julius Herford. *Choral Conducting Symposium.* Englewood Cliffs, NJ: Prentice-Hall, 1988.

Demorest, Steven. "Customizing Choral Warm-ups." *The Choral Journal,* February 1993, pp. 25-28.

———. "Structuring a Musical Choral Rehearsal." *Music Educators Journal,* January 1996, p. 25.

Dickson, John. "Score Study: A Magical Eye for Musical Blueprints." *The Choral Journal,* 39-8, March 1999, p. 9.

> *Lengthy and detailed discussion of macro to micro score study, following model of Julius Herford and Margaret Hillis. Text is a primary consideration for this author. Academic and detailed, and very helpful.*

Donaldson, Robert P. "The Practice and Pedagogy of Vocal Legato." *The NATS Bulletin,* 29, 1973, pp. 12-21.

Doscher, Barbara M. *The Functional Unity of the Singing Voice.* Metuchen, NJ: The Scarecrow Press, 1988.

Duarte, F. "The Principles of Alexander Technique Applied to Singing: The Significance of the Preparatory Set." *Journal of Research in Singing,* 5-1, pp. 3-21.

Ehmann, Wilhelm. *Choral Directing.* Minneapolis, MN: Augsburg Publishing House, 1968.

———. "Performance Practice of Bach's Motets." *American Choral Review,* VII, September 1964, 4-5; December 1964, 6-7; March 1965, 6; and June 1965), 8-12.

Ehmann, Wilhelm, and Frauke Haasemann. *Voice Building for Choirs.* Chapel Hill, NC: Hinshaw Music, Inc., 1982.

Eichenberger, Rodney. *Enhancing Musicality Through Movement.* Santa Barbara, CA: Santa Barbara Music.

———. *What You See Is What You Get.* (Video) Chapel Hill, NC: Hinshaw Music, Inc.

Ericson, Eric. *Choral Conducting.* New York: Walton Music Corporation: 1976.

Eustis, Lynn. *When Singers Become Voice Teachers.* Chicago: GIA Publications, 2013.

Feder, R.J. "Vocal Health: A View from the Medical Profession. *The Choral Journal,* 30-7, pp. 23-25.

Finn, William J. *The Art of the Choral Conductor.* Vol. I and II. Evanston, IL: Summy-Birchard Company, 1960.

———. *The Conductor Raises His Baton.* New York: Harper and Brothers, 1944.

Fisher, R.E. "Choral Diction with a Phonological Foundation." *The Choral Journal,* 27-5, pp. 13-18.

Fowler, Charles, ed. *Conscience of a Profession: Howard Swan.* Chapel Hill, NC: Hinshaw Music, Inc., 1987.

Frisell, Anthony. *The Baritone Voice.* Boston, MA: Crescendo Publishers, 1972.

———. *The Soprano Voice.* Boston. MA: Bruce Humphries, 1966.

———. *The Tenor Voice.* Boston, MA: Bruce Humphries, 1964.

Fuchs, Peter Paul. *The Psychology of Conducting.* New York: MCA, 1969.

Fuchs, Viktor. *The Art of Singing and Voice Technique.* New York: London House and Maxwell, 1964.

Gackle, Lynn. *Finding Ophelia's Voice, Opening Ophelia's Heart: Nurturing the Adolescent Female Voice.* Heritage Music Press, 2011 (paperback). Includes a DVD.

———. "The Adolescent Female Voice: Characteristics of Change and Stages of Development. *The Choral Journal,* 31-8, pp. 17-25.

Gajard, Dom Joseph. *The Solesmes Method.* Collegeville, MN: The Liturgical Press, 1960.

Garcia, Manuel. *A Complete Treatise on the Art of Singing.* Trans. Donald V. Paschke. New York: Da Capo Press, 1972.

Garretson, Robert L. "The Singer s Posture and the Circulatory System." *The Choral Journal,* April 1990, p.19.

Glenn, Carole, ed. *In Quest of Answers: Interviews with American Choral Conductors.* Chapel Hill, NC: Hinshaw Music, Inc, 1991.

Goetze, Mary. "Factors Affecting Accuracy in Children s Singing." *Dissertation Abstracts International,* 46, 2955A.

Gordon, Edwin E. *Advanced Measures of Music Audiation.* Chicago: GIA Publications, 1989.

———. *Intermediate Measures of Music Audiation.* Chicago: GIA Publications, 1982.

———. *Iowa Tests of Music Literacy.* Chicago: GIA Publications, 1991.

———. *Learning Sequences in Music.* Chicago: GIA Publications, 1989.

———. "Research Studies in Audiation: 1," *Council for Research in Music Education,* 84, 1985, pp. 34-35.

———. *The Nature, Description, Measurement and Evaluation of Music Aptitudes.* Chicago: GIA Publications, 1987.

Haasemann, Frauke, and Irene Willis. *Group Vocal Technique for Children's Choirs* (unpublished manuscript).

Haasemann, Frauke, and James Jordan. *Group Vocal Technique.* Chapel Hill, NC: Hinshaw Music, 1991.

———. *Group Vocal Technique: The Vocalise Cards.* Chapel Hill, NC: Hinshaw Music, 1991.

———. *Group Vocal Technique.* (Video) Chapel Hill, NC: Hinshaw Music, 1991.

> *This video is a wonderful teaching/learning tool that documents in film the teaching of Frauke Haasemann. It is higly recommended to all students of vocal technique for choirs.*

Hemsley, Thomas. *Singing and Imagination.* Oxford: Oxford University Press, 1998.

Higgins, Kathleen Marie. *The Music Between Us.* Chicago: The University of Chicago Press, 2012.

Hisley, Philip D. "Head Quality Versus Nasality: A Review of Pertinent Literature." *The NATS Bulletin,* 28, 1971, pp. 4-15.

Hofbauer, Kurt. *Praxis der Chorsichen Stimmbildung.* Mainz: Schott Verlag, 1978.

Horstmann, Sabine. *Chorische Stiimmbildung.* Merseburger Verlag, 1996.

> *This small book contains many practical and useful exercises for use in constructing a warm-up.*

Huff-Gackle, Lynne Martha. "The Adolescent Female Voice: Characteristics of Change and Stages of Development." *The Choral Journal,* pp. 31-38; March 1991, pp. 17-25.

———. "The effect of selected vocal techniques for breath management, resonation, and vowel unification on tone production in the junior high school female voice." Ph.D. dissertation, University of Miami, 1987.

Humphrey, Nicolas. *Soul Dust.* Princeton: Princeton University Press, 2011.

James, David. "Intonation Problems at the Level of the Larynx." *The NATS Bulletin,* 39, 1983, pp. 14-16.

Jordan, James. "Audiation and Sequencing: An Approach to Score Preparation." *The Choral Journal,* XXI/8, April 1981, pp. 11-13.

———. "Choral Intonation: A Pedagogical Problem for the Choral Conductor." *The Choral Journal,* April 1987.

———. *Evoking Sound: Fundamentals of Choral Conducting and Rehearsing.* Chicago: GIA Publications, 1996.

———. "False Blend: A Vocal Pedagogy Problem for the Choral Conductor." *The Choral Journal,* XXIV/10, June 1984, pp. 25-26.

———. *Learn Conducting Technique with the Swiss Exercise Ball.* Chicago: GIA Publications, 2004.

———. *The Musician's Soul.* Chicago: GIA Publications, 1999.

———. *The Musician's Spirit.* Chicago: GIA Publications, 2002.

———. "Toward a Flexible Sound Ideal Through Conducting: Some Reactions to Study with Wilhelm Ehmann." *The Choral Journal,* XXV/3, November 1984, pp. 5-6.

Jordan, James, and Marilyn Shenenberger. *Ear Training Immersion Exercises for Choirs.* Chicago: GIA Publications, 2004.

Jordan, James, and Matthew Mehaffey. *Choral Ensemble Intonation.* Chicago: GIA Publications, 2001.

Jordan, James, with Constantina Tsolainou, Craig Dennison, and Vincent Metallo. *The Choral Ensemble Warm-Up.* Chapel Hill, NC: Hinshaw Music, 1998.

Joyner, D.R. "The Monotone Problem." *Journal of Research in Music Education,* 17-1, pp. 114-125.

Judd, Percey. *Vocal Technique.* London: Sylvan Press, 1951.

Kagen, Sergius. *On Studying Singing.* New York: Dover Publications, 1960.

Keenze, Marvin H. "Singing City Choirs." *The Journal of Church Music*, X, September 1968, pp. 8-10.

Kemp, Helen. *A Helen Kemp Portrait: Insight and Inspiration from a Master Teacher of Children's Choirs.* Garland, TX: The Choristers Guild, 2001.

———. *Of Primary Importance.* Garland, TX: The Choristers Guild, 1989.

Kirk, Theron. *Choral Tone and Technique.* Westbury, NY: Pro-Art, 1956.

Klein, Joseph J. *Singing Technique: How to Avoid Vocal Trouble.* Princeton: D. VanNostrand, 1967.

Lamperti, Francesco. *The Technics of Bel Canto.* New York: G. Schirmer, 1905.

Lamperti, Giovanni Battista. *Vocal Wisdom.* New York: Taplinger Publishing Company, 1957.

Landeau, Michael. "Voice Classification." *The NATS Bulletin*, October 1963, pp. 4-8.

Large, John, Edward Baird, and Timothy Jenkins. "Studies of Male Voice Mechanisms: Preliminary Report and Definition of the Term Register." *Journal of Research in Singing*, 4, 1981, pp. 1-26.

Leck, Henry. *The Boy's Changing Voice.* (Video) Hal Leonard, Inc.

Lieberman, Phillip. *Intonation, Perception and Language.* Cambridge, MA: The MIT Press, 1967.

Mari, Nanda. *Canto e voce.* Milan: G. Ricordi, 1970.

Marshall, Madeleine. *The Singer's Manual of English Diction.* New York: G. Schirmer, 1963.

Mason, Lowell. *Manual of the Boston Academy of Music for Instruction in the Elements of Vocal Music on the System of Pestalozzi.* Boston, MA: J.H. Wilkins and R.B. Carfter, 1839.

McCoy, Scott. *Your Voice: An Inside View.* Inside View Press, 2012. McKinney, James. The Diagnosis and Correction of Vocal Faults. Nashville, TN: Broadman Press, 1982.

Miller, Donald. *Resonance in Singing: Voice Building through Acoustic Feedback.* Inside View Press, 2008.

Miller, Kenneth C. *Principles of Singing.* Englewood Cliffs, NJ: Prentice-Hall, 1983.

Miller, Richard. *English, French, German and Italian Techniques of Singing.* Metuchen, NJ: Scarecrow Press, 1977.

———. *On the Art of Singing*. New York: Oxford, 1996.

———. "The Solo Singer in the Choral Ensemble." *The Choral Journal*, March 1995.

———. *The Structure of Singing*. New York: Schirmer Books, 1986. Miller,

———. *Training Soprano Voices*. New York: Oxford University Press, 2000.

———. *Training Tenor Voices*. New York: Schirmer Books, 1993.

Moe, Daniel. *Basic Choral Concepts*. Minneapolis, MN: Augsburg, 1968.

Montini, Nicola A. *The Correct Pronunciation of Latin According to Roman Usage*. Chicago: GIA Publications, 1973.

Moore, Thomas. *Care of the Soul*. New York: Harper-Perennial, 1992.

Moriarty, John. *Diction: Italian, Latin, French and German*. Boston, MA: E.C. Schirmer, 1975.

Palmer, Parker. *A Hidden Wholeness*. San Francisco, CA: Jossey-Bass, 2004.

Phillips, Kenneth. *Teaching Kids to Sing*. New York: G. Schirmer, 1992.

Phillips, Kenneth H. "The effects of group breath control training on selected vocal measures related to the singing ability of children in grades two, three and four." Ph.D. Dissertation, Kent State University, 1983.

Proctor, Donald. *Breathing, Speech and Song*. New York: Springer-Verlag, 1980.

Pysh, Gregory M. "Chorophony: The Art of Father Finn." *The Choral Journal*, November 1996, p. 37.

Rao, Doreen. *Choral Music Experience, Vol. I: Artistry in Music Education*. New York: Boosey & Hawkes, 1987.

———. *Choral Music Experience, Vol. 2: The Young Singing Voice*. New York: Boosey & Hawkes, 1987.

Reid, Cornelius L. *The Free Voice: A Guide to Natural Singing*. New York: Joseph Patelson Music House, 1965.

———. *Voice: Psyche and Soma*. New York: Joseph Patelson Music House, 1965.

Roberts, E., and A. Davies. "The Response of Monotones to a Program of Remedial Training," *Journal of Research in Music Education*, 1975, 23, 4, pp. 227-239.

Robinson, Ray. "Wilhelm Ehmann's Approach to Choral Training." *The Choral Journal*, November 1984, pp. 5-7.

Robinson, R., and A. Winold. *The Choral Experience*. New York: Harper's College Press, 1976.

Robinson, Russell. *Creative Rehearsal Techniques*. (Video) Warner Brothers Music.

Rose, Arnold. *The Singer and the Voice*. New York: St. Martin's Press, 1971.

Rushmore, Robert. *The Singing Voice*. New York: Dodd and Mead, 1971.

Sable, Barbara Kinsey. *The Vocal Sound*. Englewood Cliffs, NJ: Prentice-Hall, Inc., 1982.

Sataloff, R.T. "Ten Good Ways to Abuse Your Voice: A Singer s Guide to a Short Career." *The NATS Journal*, (Part 1) 42-1, pp. 23-25.

———. "Ten Good Ways to Abuse Your Voice: A Singer s Guide to a Short Career." *The NATS Journal*, (Part 2) 43-1, pp. 22-26.

Sataloff, R.T., and J.R. Spiegel. "The Young Voice." *The NATS Journal*, 45 (3), 1989, pp. 35-37.

Scott, Anthony. "Acoustic Pecularities of Head Tone and Falsetto." *The NATS Bulletin*, 33, 1974, pp. 32-35.

Seashore, Carl E. *The Psychology of Musical Talent*. Boston, MA: Silver-Burdett, 1919.

Sellars-Young, Barbara. *Breathing Movement Exploration*. New York: Applause Books, 2001.

Shaw, Robert. "Letters to a Symphony Chorus." *The Choral Journal*, April 1986, pp. 5-8.

Shaw, Robert. *Preparing a Masterpiece: Volume I, The Brahms Requiem*. (Video) New York: Carnegie Hall.

> *This valuable video contains a wonderful overview of Mr. Shaw's philosophies and rehearsal techniques. It is available only through the Carnegie Hall Gift Shop or carnegiehall.org.*

Shuter-Dyson, Rosamund, and Clive Gabriel. *The Psychology of Musical Ability*. London: Methuen, 1981.

Stark, James. *Bel Canto: A History of Vocal Pedagogy*. Toronto: University of Toronto Press, 2003.

Stransky, J., and R.B. Stone. *Joy in the Life of Your Body*. New York: Beaufort, 1981.

Sundberg, Johann. *The Science of the Singing Voice*. DeKalb, IL: Northern Illinois University Press, 1987.

Sunderman, Lloyd Frederick. *Artistic Singing: Its Tone Production and Basic Understandings.* Metuchen, NJ: Scarecrow Press, Inc., 1970.

Swanson, Frederick J. "The Changing Voice." *The Choral Journal,* March 1976, pp. 5-14.

——. *The Male Singing Voice Ages Eight to Eighteen.* Cedar Rapids, IA: Laurence Press, 1977.

Swears, Linda. *Teaching the Elementary School Chorus.* West Nyack, NY: Parker, 1985.

Taff, Merle E. "An Acoustic Study of Vowel Modification and Register Transition in the Male Singing Voice." *The NATS Bulletin,* 22, 1965, pp. 8-35.

Taggart, Cynthia Crump. "The Measurement and Evaluation of Music Aptitudes and Achievement." In *Source Readings in Music Learning Theory.* Darrel Walters and Cynthia Crump Taggart, eds. Chicago: GIA Publications, 1989, pp. 45-55.

Thomas, Franz. *Bel Canto.* Berlin: George Achterberg Verlag, 1968.

Thomas, Kurt. *The Choral Conductor.* New York: Associated Music Publishers, 1971.

Thurmond, James Morgan. *Note Grouping.* Camp Hill, PA: JMT Publications, 1989.

Treash, Leonard. "The Importance of Vowel Sounds and Their Modification in Producing Good Tone." *The NATS Bulletin,* 4, (1943), p. 3.

Tsolainou, Constantina, and James Jordan. *Ensemble Diction.* (Video) Chapel Hill, NC: Hinshaw Music, 1998.

Vennard, William. *Developing Voices.* New York: Carl Fischer, Inc., 1973.

——. *Singing: The Mechanism and the Technic.* Revised edition. New York: Carl Fischer, Inc., 1967.

Waengler, Hans Heinrich. "Some Remarks and Observations on the Function of the Soft Palate." *The NATS Bulletin,* 25, 1968, p. 24.

Wall, Joan. *Diction for Singers.* Dallas, TX: Pst..., Inc, 1990.

——. *International Phonetic Alphabet for Singers.* Dallas, TX: Pst..., Inc. 1989.

Waring, F. *Tone Syllables.* Delaware Water Gap, PA: Shawnee Press, 1951.

Webb, Guy, ed. *Up Front!* Boston, MA: E.C. Schirmer, 1994.

Weikart, Phyllis. *Teaching Movement and Dance: A Sequential Approach to Rhythmic Movement.* Yipsalanti, MI: High Scope Press, 1989.

Williamson, John Finley. "Choral Singing" (articles individually titled).
   Twelve articles in Etude, LXVIII and LXIX (April 1950-October 1951).
———. "Training the Individual Voice Through Choral Singing." *Proceedings*
   of the Music Teachers National Association, XXXIII, 1938, pp. 52-59.
Wright, E. *Basic Choir Training.* Croydon, England. The Royal School of
   Church Music, 1955.
Zemlin, Willard R. *Speech and Hearing Science.* Englewood Cliffs, NJ:
   Prentice-Hall, Inc., 1988.

TEXT TRANSLATION RESOURCES

Jeffers, Ron. *Translations and Annotations of Sacred German Texts.*
   Corvalis, OR, 1996.
———. *Translations and Annotations of Sacred Latin Texts.* Corvalis, OR:
   Earthsongs, 1988.

BODY MAPPING RESOURCES

Conable, Barbara, and William Conable. *How to Learn the Alexander Technique:*
   A Manual for Students. Portland, OR: Andover Press, 1995.
Conable, Barbara. *The Structures and Movement of Breathing.* Chicago:
   GIA Publications, 2000.
———. *What Every Musician Needs to Know About the Body.*
   Portland, OR: Andover Press.
      This is a book about Body Mapping and the kinesthetic sense and how
      they can be developed in ways that help musicians play well. It is full
      of information about the Alexander Technique, but it is very useful for
      people who don't have access to an Alexander teacher as well.
Jordan, James, and Heather Buchanan. *Body Mapping and Basic Conducting*
   Patterns. (Video and DVD) Chicago: GIA Publications, 2002.

DICTION RESOURCES

Cheek,Timothy. *Singing in Czech.* London: The Scarecrow Press, 2001.
Farish, Stephen. *French Diction for Singers.* Denton, TX: Gore Publishing
   Company, 1999.

Grubb, Thomas. *Singing in French*. New York: Schirmer, 1979.

Hines, Robert S. *Singer's Manual of Latin Diction and Phonetics*. London: Collier Macmillian Publishers, 1975.

Marshall, Madeleine. *The Singer's Manual of English Diction*. New York: G. Schirmer, 1963.

McGee, Timothy J. *Singing Early Music: The Pronunciation of European Languages in the Late Middle Ages and Renaissance*. Bloomington, IN: Indiana University Press, 1996.

Moriarty, John. *Diction: Italian, Latin, French and German*. Boston, MA: E.C. Schirmer, 1975.

ANATOMICAL MODEL RESOURCES

Anatomy.com website.
> *Company that markets anatomical models for use in Body Mapping instruction.*

APTITUDE TESTING

Gordon, Edwin E. *Advanced Measures of Music Audiation*. Chicago: GIA Publications.

———. *Intermediate Measures of Music Audiation*. Chicago: GIA Publications.

———. *Primary Measures of Music Audiation*. Chicago: GIA Publications.

WEBSITES

Bodymap.org website. Website of Barbara Conable.
GIAmusic.com website. Website of GIA Publications, Inc.
Hinshawmusic.com website. Website of Hinshaw Music.
Voiceinsideview.com website.
> *Website for information concerning Your Voice: An Inside View of Multimedia Voice Science and Pedagogy by Scott McCoy. A tremendous resource to assist in Body Mapping the vocal apparatus for your choir. The book and CD-ROM is a multimedia exploration of voice science and pedagogy, among the first pedagogical textbooks to*

make extensive use of audio, video, and high-resolution photographic examples. This is achieved through an interactive computer program designed to be used as a standalone application. A traditional printed text that references examples from the computer program is also available. The program runs directly from a CD-ROM or can be installed on the hard drive of your personal computer. Available for PC and MAC. CD-ROM includes: 150+ video examples, 85 audio examples, 100 photos & drawings, including images from the Netter Collection and the Rohen Atlas of Anatomy Roll-over identification of anatomical features—point the mouse to a structure, its name and function will pop up. This CD-ROM available with a print version textbook.

ABOUT THE AUTHORS

JAMES JORDAN

GRAMMY®-nominated conductor James Jordan is recognized and praised around the world as one of America's preeminent conductors, writers, recording artists, and innovators in choral music. The most published author in the choral world, his 35 books form the canon for teaching conductors and choirs worldwide. He was described as a "visionary" by *The Choral Journal*, which has cited his book *Evoking Sound* as a "must read." He is Professor and Senior Conductor at Westminster Choir College of Rider University, where he conducts the Westminster Schola Cantorum and the internationally acclaimed Westminster Williamson Voices. He is also conductor/artistic director of The Same Stream (thesamestreamchoir.com), a group of singers with a shared experience through their education at Westminster Choir College. Their inaugural recording, *The Same Stream*, presents the music of Thomas LaVoy and features the world-premiere recording of *Songs of the Questioner*.

Dr. Jordan studied with the legendary conductors and scholars of the past 40 years, including Elaine Brown, Wilhelm Ehmann, Frauke Haasemann, Volker Hempfling, and renowned music psychologist Edwin Gordon. His career as a conductor began as a finalist in the Leopold Stokowski Conducting Competition with The Philadelphia Orchestra under Eugene Ormandy. Educated both as a conductor and a music psychologist, Dr. Jordan is uniquely qualified to bring varying perspectives regarding the choral art to conductors and teachers.

Dr. Jordan has made two recordings of the music of James Whitbourn with the Westminster Williamson Voices on the Naxos label, which have garnered wide critical acclaim on both sides of the Atlantic. *Gramophone* hailed him as a conductor of "forceful and intimate choral artistry," and regarding the GRAMMY®-nominated recording of *Annelies, Choir and Organ* wrote,

"Jordan's instinctive understanding of the score makes this a profound and emotionally charged experience." The Westminster Williamson Voices, acclaimed on both sides of the Atlantic by reviewers and composers alike for their compelling sound and artistry, premiered over 40 choral works by the world's leading composers, among them Jaakko Mantyjaarvi, Blake Henson, Gerald Custer, Thomas LaVoy, Cortlandt Matthews, Dan Forrest, Paul Mealor, and James Whitbourn.

Dr. Jordan's residencies, master classes, and guest conducting have taken him throughout the United States, Canada, Europe, and Australia. He has taught master classes at The Curtis Institute, Rhoades College, The University of North Texas, University of Buffalo, Temple University, University of Arizona, University of Aberdeen, and the U.S. Army Soldiers Chorus. He has conducted more than 30 all-state choirs. In 2009, he was named to the choral panel for The National Endowment for the Arts. He serves as director of the Westminster Conducting Institute (rider.edu/ConductingInstitute), one of the nation's leading summer programs for the training and education of conductors, and co-director with James Whitbourn of the Westminster Choral Institute at Oxford (rider.edu/Oxford), a unique partnership with St. Stephen's House, one of the Halls of Oxford University. Since its establishment in 2013, this program has quickly established itself as one of the world's recognized programs for the teaching of choral artistry to choral conductors.

Dr. Jordan's career and publications have been devoted to innovative educational changes in the choral art, which have been embraced around the world. His writings have shaped far-reaching changes in the philosophy of music teaching and learning, conducting pedagogy, and the teaching of rhythm applying Laban Effort/Shape to both music teaching and conducting. In 2012, he received the Iorio Research Prize from Rider University. His exclusive publisher is GIA Publications in Chicago (giamusic.com), and he is Executive Editor of the Evoking Sound Choral Series (GIA), an extensive catalog of almost 200 works representing one of the largest and most comprehensive choral series in world. His most recent publications, *Discovering Chant, Sound as Teacher,* and *The Musician's Breath* have received wide critical acclaim.

Dr. Jordan has been honored as a distinguished alumnus at both Susquehanna University and Temple University. He was awarded the distinguished Doctor of Music by the University of Aberdeen in Scotland in 2014 to honor his contributions to choral music throughout the world. Only the second American since 1485 to receive this degree, he shares this honor with Gustav Holst, Benjamin Britten, Dame Joan Sutherland, and Morten Lauridsen.

SEAN MCCARTHER

Sean McCarther serves as Assistant Professor of Voice at Westminster Choir College, where he teaches studio voice, voice science, and movement for performers. He holds a DM and MM from Indiana University with an emphasis in vocal pedagogy, postural analysis, and movement for the stage.

Dr. McCarther has presented scholarly research at the the Dalcroze Society of America, NATS 53rd National Conference, NATS Eastern Regional Conference, Indiana Music Teachers Association, and several other local and regional conferences. Other publications include a two-part article for the *Journal of Singing* on postural analysis and body alignment.

An advocate for physical theater and mobile singers, Dr. McCarther has created a movement-based performance pedagogy called Body, Mind, and Voice (BMV) Performance Training. The training draws upon a multitude of movement disciplines to create a multifaceted movement pedagogy that frees the body from unnecessary tension; allows both effortless movement and easy, organic phonation; and helps students learn to actively engage their environment, their scene partners, and the audience with the highest potential expression. He has presented BMV workshops at Westminster Choir College, the University of Texas, and Baylor University. He is also on the faculty of the CoOPERAtive Program at Westminster Choir College as a movement instructor.

KATHY KESSLER PRICE

Kathy Kessler Price, Ph.D., is an Associate Professor of Voice at Westminster Choir College, where she teaches voice lessons and courses in voice pedagogy, and directs the Presser Voice Lab. Formerly, she taught at Mississippi State University, William Jewell College, and Northern Virginia Community College. She is a founding member of the Washington Vocal Consortium and conductor/ artistic director of the women's ensemble, Philomela, both in the Washington, DC area. A native Virginian, she began her studies in voice performance and music education at the University of Richmond, continued at the University of Maryland, where she attained her Master of Music in Voice Performance, and completed her PhD in Voice Pedagogy at The University of Kansas.

As a soprano, Dr. Price has performed as soloist in such distinguished venues as The Kennedy Center, Carnegie Hall, The National Museum for Women in the Arts, the Embassy of the Czech Republic, and The White House. She performed as a member of the Washington National Opera chorus for twelve years, six under the artistic direction of Plácido Domingo. Her title roles include Smetana's *The Bartered Bride,* Lehar's *The Merry Widow,* and Herbert's *Naughty Marietta,* as well as Miss Silverpeal in Mozart's *The Impresario,* Lucy in Menotti's *The Telephone,* and leading roles in numerous Gilbert and Sullivan operettas and musical theater. She is a frequent soloist in oratorio, concert, and recital, where she champions contemporary composers. She has toured the Czech Republic as a recitalist and served as a performer and clinician in Brazil, Russia, and Croatia.

Dr. Price's research presentations include menopausal and aging voices, the efficacy of voice assessments in a conservatory setting, voice studio technology use, breathing task measurements, and comparative differences in musical theater and Classical female voices. In 2010, she received the Voice Pedagogy Award from the National Association of Teachers of Singing. She is founder and director of Westminster Choir College's annual Voice Pedagogy Institute, which trains teachers in fact-based voice teaching. She is published in the *Journal of Singing* and the *Journal of Research in Music Education,* among others.

COREY EVERLY

Corey Everly is a collaborative pianist, coach, and conductor. He holds a master's degree from Westminster Choir College in piano accompanying and coaching, where he studied with Dr. J. J. Penna. He has previously been accompanist for the GRAMMY®-nominated Westminster Williamson Voices and the Westminster Schola Cantorum, and he is currently Assistant Artistic Director and accompanist for The Same Stream Choir (James Jordan, conductor). He has conducted over thirty musical theatre/opera productions spanning a wide range of styles. He holds a bachelor's degree in voice performance from Westminster Choir College, where he studied with Faith Esham, and he maintains a private piano and voice studio in Philadelphia, Pennsylvania. He is on the theatre faculty of Rowan University and the piano and voice faculty at Cornerstone Music Studios in Millstone, New Jersey. As a chorister, he has sung with leading conductors such as Yannick Nézet-Séguin, Simon Rattle, Daniele Gatti, and Gustavo Dudamel. Highlights include the Verdi *Requiem* and the Mahler *Symphony No. 2* with the Philadelphia Orchestra in Carnegie Hall and performances with the Simon Bolivar Symphony Orchestra, also at Carnegie Hall. One of his favorite projects to date includes performances of the Bernstein *Mass* with the Philadelphia Orchestra and Yannick Nézet-Séguin.

JONATHAN PALMER LAKELAND

Jonathan Palmer Lakeland, hailing from the United States, is a piano accompanist working with singers across the world. His playing has been described as "pointed and dramatic" (Robert Hugill, PlanetHugill), and as "wordless eloquence...he supported the singers with both brio and sensitivity, clearly relishing his involvement in the dramatic narrative" (Margaret Tattersall, *The Herald*, Stratford-upon-Avon). He has performed with soloists and choirs in venues across the world. Most recently, he completed a concert tour of Ghana, performing in the Great Hall, Kwame Nkrumah University of Science and Technology in Kumasi, Ghana; the American Embassy in Accra, Ghana; and Obama Hall at the Palace of Osabarima Kwasi Atta II (Chief of Cape Coast, Ghana) in a private performance for the Chief and his family.

From 2010 to 2014, he served as the principal accompanist of the GRAMMY®-nominated Westminster Williamson Voices. He has been a longtime collaborator of conductor James Jordan. Together, they have collaborated on numerous concert, recording, literary, and educational projects. He continues this collaboration today in many ways, including as a part of the Choral Institute at Oxford each summer. He has served on the music staff of the Georg Solti Accademia in Castilgione della Pescaia, Italy, accompanying and coaching singers in bel canto repertoire alongside faculty Jonathan Papp, Maestro Richard Bonynge, Angela Gheorghiu, Carmen Gianattasio, and others. He has also coached singers at the Royal Academy Opera, Royal Academy of Music, and Westminster Choir College.

He has studied conducting with Sian Edwards, Paul Brough, and James Jordan, and has worked on the conducting staff of opera companies in both

Europe and the United States. He also serves as Executive Director of The Same Stream, a professional choir led by artistic director James Jordan. He trained with Malcolm Martineau, Julius Drake, James Baillieu, and Michael Dussek at the Royal Academy of Music in London; with Maestro Richard Bonynge and Jonathan Papp at the Solti Accademia's répétiteur course in Venice, Italy; and with JJ Penna and James Goldsworthy at Westminster Choir College in Princeton, New Jersey.